SINGAPORE HERITAGE COOKBOOKS

EURASIAN HERITAGE
Cooking

SINGAPORE HERITAGE COOKBOOKS

EURASIAN HERITAGE
Cooking

QUENTIN PEREIRA
Foreword by MICHAEL PALMER

mc **Marshall Cavendish**
Cuisine

Editor: Lydia Leong
Designer: Bernard Go
Photographer: Hongde Photography

Copyright © 2012 Marshall Cavendish International (Asia) Private Limited

This book is supported under the National Heritage Board's
Heritage Industry Incentive Programme (Hi²P)

Published by Marshall Cavendish Cuisine
An imprint of Marshall Cavendish International

Other Marshall Cavendish Offices:

Marshall Cavendish Corporation. 99 White Plains Road, Tarrytown NY 10591-9001, USA · Marshall
Cavendish International (Thailand) Co Ltd. 253 Asoke, 12th Flr, Sukhumvit 21 Road, Klongtoey Nua,
Wattana, Bangkok 10110, Thailand · Marshall Cavendish (Malaysia) Sdn Bhd, Times Subang, Lot 46,
Subang Hi-Tech Industrial Park, Batu Tiga, 40000 Shah Alam, Selangor Darul Ehsan, Malaysia

Marshall Cavendish is a trademark of Times Publishing Limited

National Library Board, Singapore Cataloguing-in-Publication Data

Pereira, Quentin.
Eurasian heritage cooking / Quentin Pereira. – Singapore : Marshall Cavendish Cuisine, c2012.
p. cm.
ISBN : 978-981-4346-46-7

1. Cooking, Singaporean. 2. Eurasians – Singapore – Social life and customs – History. I. Title. II. Series:
Singapore heritage cookbooks.

TX724.5.S55
641.595957 -- dc23   OCN795858673

Printed in Singapore by KWF Printing Pte Ltd

DEDICATION

To my mum Freda Pereira and my dad Robin Pereira, for their guidance, patience, understanding and support these past 40 years. Their teachings, influence and mass experience have made me what I am today.

To my beloved wife Kristine and son Khaell, for their inspiration and support, and for always being there for me.

Quentin Pereira

CONTENTS

FOREWORD

I am honoured to have been invited to provide this foreword. I was approached by Quentin several months ago to provide a foreword for a collection of Eurasian recipes that he was putting together for a cookbook. To facilitate this, Quentin was kind enough to provide me with a sneak peek of this book, *Eurasian Heritage Cooking*.

Contained in these pages is one of the most exciting collections of recipes for delectable Eurasian cooking that one can find. I have had the privilege of tasting Quentin's cooking on more than one occasion and I am sure that these recipes will provide a good sampling of the talent and skill that makes Quentin's The Eurasian Restaurant one of the best restaurants for Eurasian food in Singapore.

What I found particularly refreshing about this book is the richness in its representation of Eurasian culture. The cuisine of a people embodies and manifests the culture of that people, and in representing the culture of the Eurasian people in his recipes, Quentin has taken care in the introduction of the book to explain the origin of that culture and its genesis.

2011 marked the 500th year of Eurasians in the Asian region. While it is important for us to look ahead to our future, we should not underestimate our history and the significant impact that it has had in the region. In today's globalised world, the Eurasian culture and people stand out as global citizens, the origins of which started 500 years ago. A part of that culture is captured in the pages of this book.

Bon Apétit! Bom Apetite! Smakelijk Eten! Enjoy!

Michael Palmer

D.MANUEL I

LISBOA
SEC. XVI

ACKNOWLEDGEMENTS

I would like to thank Speaker of Parliament Mr Michael Palmer for taking time off his busy schedule to contribute the foreword to this book; the Eurasian Association Singapore, in particular, Burton Westerhout and Jacqueline Peeris, for providing valuable insight into the culture and heritage of the Singapore Eurasians through writing the introduction to this book; and Yvonne Pereira of the Eurasian Association and Lydia Leong of Marshall Cavendish for helping me to put this book together to preserve the Eurasian heritage, culture and recipes for future generations.

Quentin Pereira

INTRODUCTION

The term Eurasian has been in use since the mid 19th century, during British rule in India. The British coined the term to define a person born to a British father and an Indian mother, and it was officially used in the Straits Settlements records in 1849. Today, the term is used to refer to a person who has both European and Asian parentage. The Eurasians in Singapore can trace their origins to various trading ports in the region where Europeans have settled, including Malacca, Penang, Bencoolen, Goa, Ceylon and Macau.

Of Portuguese Heritage

In the 14th century, Goa served as the seat of the Portuguese administration in India and from there, a sizeable Portuguese settlement developed. In 1511, Portugal's Viceroy of India, Afonso de Albuquerque, conquered Malacca, giving Portugal control of the main Asiatic trade routes, and Malacca remained under Portuguese control until the Dutch conquest in 1641.

On 20 December 1999, Portugal gave up its last colony in its once vast overseas empire, when Macau, reverted to China rule after 442 years. In their wake, they left their architecture, culture, Catholic faith and the progeny of marriages between the Portuguese and the local people.

During the four centuries of Portuguese rule, the tiny colony of Macau served as an important link between India, China and Japan, and a centre for Christianity in Asia. Easy movement and migration between Macau and other Portuguese colonies in the region added to the diverse ethnic mix. The Portuguese Eurasian families in Singapore with roots originating in Goa, Malacca and Macau include those with surnames such as Cardoza, de Souza, de Silva, Pinto, Albuquerque, D'Almeida, Lopez and Noronha.

Of Dutch Heritage

The Dutch had a solid presence in Ceylon (present-day Sri Lanka), dating back to 1602 with the establishment of the Dutch East India Company. The Dutch Eurasian community that grew up in Ceylon became known as the Dutch Burghers. In 1641, the Dutch conquered Malacca, wrestling it from the hands of the Portuguese. Descendants of the Dutch in Ceylon and Malacca include those with surnames such as Jansen, van Cuylenberg, Campbell, Westerhout, Minjoot and Neubronner.

Of British Heritage

After the Napoleonic wars, the Dutch Governor surrendered Malacca to the British East India Company in August 1795, signalling a period of 'swaps' between the two colonial powers until the

Unveiling the statue of Sir Thomas Stamford Raffles which was relocated to the Victoria Memorial Hall during Singapore's Centenary Celebrations on 6 February 1919. Raffles founded Singapore when he purchased the land for the British East India Company in 1819.

Steamships at New Harbour, Singapore, circa 1890. The Singapore Strait was an important shipping route between Europe and the Far East, attracting many sojourners who chose to settle in Singapore.

final handover to British rule in 1824. The East India Company's influence spread with the founding of their factory at Bencoolen in 1685 and the construction of Fort Malborough in Sumatra. Since they were only a minority on the land, they had to rely on local-born men who were English-educated and experienced as junior administrators to serve as factors, writers and merchants. Immediately after the founding of Singapore in 1819, Eurasians (mainly of British descent) were transferred under the aegis of the East India Company to serve in the administration of the fledgling settlement. They were some of the first pioneer civil servants to set the trend of Eurasians to be employed later as chief clerks and junior clerks in the service of the East India Company. Eurasian families with roots in Bencoolen include the Leicester, Nicholson and Perreau families.

Britain's long colonisation of the island attracted many British-born sojourners who, having taken the opportunity of trade and enterprise, chose to put down roots and settle in Singapore. This helped contribute to a population of Eurasian families native to Singapore, including those with surnames such as Consigliere, Clarke and Milne.

South Bridge Road in the 1900s. Electric trams (centre), set up by a British company, offered an alternative to other modes of transport such as rickshaws and gharries (bottom right corner).

The clubhouse of the Singapore Recreation Club (SRC) founded by members of the Eurasian community, circa 1900.

Finding their Niche

Divided between their European and Asian heritage, the early Eurasians never found it easy to reconcile both worlds. This encouraged the community to become close-knit as they strove to find their niche in Singapore. One result of their efforts was the Singapore Recreation Club (SRC), opened on 1 July 1883 at the Padang grounds. More than just a social and recreational club, the SRC played venue to many of its members' sporting achievements.

Another testimony to the community's efforts to support their own and make a mark on the nation is the Eurasian Association, formed in 1919 as a platform for Eurasians to show a unified front and presence in the community. The Association also provided opportunities in education and acted as a channel for social and cultural activities.

When 12 Eurasian women were denied entry to the then male-dominated sports clubs, they formed the Goldburn Sports Club (later renamed the Girls' Sports Club) in July 1929. An inspirational hub, the Girls' Sports Club enabled women to participate in sporting opportunities that were only open to men at that time.

Eurasian Neighbourhoods

Like the other ethnic groups in Singapore, the early Eurasian community lived in proximity to each other in communal areas where strong bonds were forged and their group identity was strengthened.

Since the early 1850s, Eurasians lived in the residential area of Kampong Glam, specifically bounded by the areas of Waterloo Street and Queen Street. As development on the island progressed, Eurasian families moved to municipal quarters in Kampong Java and Newton, government quarters in Bukit Timah, and countryside areas of Serangoon and Upper Serangoon. The popular seaside retreat, the East Coast area of Katong, soon became a desirable residential location for many, together with the area near Selegie Road and the kampongs in Haig Road and Siglap.

Another Eurasian enclave was the area bounded by Farrer Park, Norfolk Road and Rangoon Road which was known as Little England as the roads were named after English counties and towns (names which remain even till today). In the 1920s, the area was a middle-class housing estate, each cordoned by its own compound and garden. Families would have their own gharry or horse carriage and the outhouses accommodated the syce or driver as well as the jinricksha puller who ferried the children to school.

A European style bungalow in Katong, circa 1900.

Two children in a coconut plantation in Katong, circa 1906.

A jetty made of wood and attap along the east coast of Singapore, circa 1900.

In the 1930s, Upper Serangoon was characterised by wooded estates, plantation-type houses and thatched roof bungalows. Road names were synonymous with the terrain, bearing names like Highland, Lowland, Palm Grove and Hillside, while lanes and avenues were named after resident families such as Lange, Jansen, Richards, Surin, Aroozoo and Da Silva.

A Role to Play

Since the founding of Singapore in 1819, a steady stream of Eurasians has contributed significantly to the progress of Singapore's socio-political environment. In the days of colonial rule, Eurasians with their better command of the English language held clerical and administrative positions in British offices, playing the crucial role of acquainting the British with local customs.

Though these job opportunities meant typical Eurasian families were slightly better off than most Chinese, Malay and Indian families of that time, they were nevertheless also segregated from the British social system. Even until the early 1900s, Eurasian volunteers were not given the proper distinction of an infantry company to call their own within the Singapore Volunteer Corps (SVC), a volunteer military group formed by the British colonial government in 1854. (The SVC existed through the 1960s, eventually becoming the foundation of the present day Singapore Army.) There were separate British, Chinese and Malay infantry companies, but the Eurasian and Indian volunteers were spread throughout the SVC. While proudly defending Singapore, the community also strove for equal recognition, and the inception of the first Eurasian Infantry Company, the D Company, on 4 July 1918 remains today as a nationalistic symbol of Eurasian pride and loyalty. The opportunity to defend the colony of Singapore alongside their Chinese, Malay, Indian and British counterparts came in early 1942, ending with the fall of Singapore to the Japanese forces.

During the Japanese Occupation (1942–1945), a total of about 2,000 Eurasians, including some Chinese Catholics, were relocated to set up a settlement called Fuji Village near Bahau in Negri Sembilan, Malaya. The idea was mooted by the Japanese authorities to ease the food shortage in Singapore and the settlers were encouraged to cultivate the land for their own food. The idea failed however, as many of the settlers did not have knowledge of farming and were thus unable to cultivate their own food. As a result, many suffered from malnutrition. The poor living conditions also caused many to be plagued with malaria and other diseases. Only three-quarters of the population survived to return to Singapore after the surrender of the Japanese.

The instability of post-war years after the Japanese Occupation and the continuous bias of Eurasians not being considered as European further aggravated anti-colonial sentiments, and this led

Quentin's mother, Freda (right), watching a neighbour prepare banana fritters in Kampong Serani, a Eurasian enclave, circa 1950.

to the movement of the Eurasians seeking greater self-determination and identity as a community. The years before and after Singapore gained independence in 1965 saw many notable Eurasians involved in building the foundation of the nation's administration. Many prominent Eurasians held key roles which contributed to Singapore's fledgling independence and nationhood. Amongst them were Edmund William Barker (1920–2001), Minister of Law, who authored the Independence Note of Separation, Sir George Edward Noel Oehlers (1908–1968), Speaker of the Legislative Assembly of Singapore (precursor to present Parliament), Stanley Toft Stewart (1910–1992) who was Head of Civil Service, George Edwin Bogaars (1926–1992) who was the Director of Special Branch, and John Le Cain (1912–1993), the Commissioner of Police. Notably, the foregoing were the first local citizens to hold such senior posts after Independence.

In January 1971, Dr Benjamin Henry Sheares (1907–1981), a prominent Professor of Medicine, was awarded the highest honour in the land when he was appointed the second president of the Republic of Singapore.

Eurasians consistently punched above their weight when it came to representing the nation at sports. They formed the backbone of the national soccer, hockey and cricket teams with legendary sportsmen like Noel Hay (hockey and cricket), Wilfred Skinner (soccer and hockey), Reggie da Silva (cricket), Percy Pennefather (hockey), Rudy Mosbergen (hockey) and Douglas Nonis (soccer and

The Singapore Recreation Club's first hockey team, 1950.

Mary Klass (bib number 260) at the finishing line of the 100-metre dash at the Asian Olympics in Manila, 1954.

hockey) leading the way. In 1956, the Singapore Hockey Team, which included seven Eurasians, took eighth place at the Olympic Games held in Melbourne, Australia. Individual sports personalities who won national, regional and Asian honours included Fred de Souza (shooting), Mary Klass (athletics) and Austin Dunsford (boxing).

Colourful Language

Eurasian speak is set quite apart from other ethnic tongues as it possesses a distinct flavour that includes words and phrases from the Anglo-Indian and Malaccan Portuguese patois and Malay language. As Malay has been the lingua franca of the Malay Archipelago for centuries, it is common for the Eurasians to sprinkle Malay words generously in their speech. Eurasians who trace their roots back to Malacca are familiar with the Kristang language, which evolved from the Portuguese language in the Malay Peninsula.

Since the majority of the Eurasian community is of the Roman Catholic faith, biblical references are usually found in Eurasian speech. Religious occasions and festivities are also referred to and spoken of frequently. Given their love of euphemisms, analogies and figures of speech, the Eurasian language is both lively and imaginative.

Some Kristang words found in Eurasian speech include *asi kit eng*, an expression similar to *oh my* and *muitu merseh* meaning *thank you*. Clever use of the English language and a dash of characteristic Eurasian wit has resulted in such phrases as *easier to get the Queen*, which expresses frustration at failing to get in touch with someone after countless attempts and *face like the back of the bus* when describing someone with an unpleasant disposition.

Rites, Religion and Celebrations

Drawing upon their unique heritage of a mix of many different cultures, Eurasians have come to develop and foster a culture they can truly call their own. Most Eurasian traditions are established from the Roman Catholic faith and religious symbols are found in most homes. Traditional Christian festivals such as Lent, Easter Sunday and Christmas Day are also strictly observed. The celebration of Christmas in December is by far the most important event for most Eurasians, and it is often celebrated with a mix of traditional European practices with a distinct local touch. Preparations begin early with the purchase or tailoring of new clothes. Homes would then be spring-cleaned and given a fresh coat of paint.

Enjoying party games at a family gathering, circa 1970.

In the kitchens, a festive storm would be cooked up, with many homemakers baking cakes and tarts, and preparing *acar* and curry *feng* from their own family recipes. Children would be encouraged to behave well and to write to Santa Claus. On Christmas Eve, children would hang a stocking by their bedside which would be filled with gifts from Santa Claus. Some fathers may take on the role of Santa to host Christmas parties and hand out treats.

Christmas observances begin by attending midnight Mass dressed in new clothes on 24 December. Supper at home would then follow. Typically, *tim* soup (page 56) made with pig's trotters and sour plums would be served with bread, ham, chicken pie and wine. Christmas gifts would be exchanged among members of the family. On Christmas day, a lunch would be served, typically consisting of roast turkey, curry devil, curry *feng* and bread, with rich desserts such as fruit cake, sugee cake (page 166) and pineapple tarts (page 142) to complete the meal.

Another significant date in the calendar for the Eurasians is Easter Sunday, which is preceded by Holy Week beginning with Palm Sunday. On this day, palm leaves are distributed to members of the congregation to commemorate the entrance of Christ into Jerusalem. On the night of Maundy Thursday, Catholics would attend Mass and then visit at least three churches.

Good Friday would then begin with a hearty breakfast of hot cross buns, black coffee and *kueh ko chee* (page 146), a snack which is also served during funeral wakes. At three in the afternoon,

A Eurasian family having a casual family meal of bread and curry, circa 1980.

families would attend the Veneration of the Cross service. Holy Week, which is observed in the last week of Lent, ends with Easter Sunday. Children enjoy this holiday with gifts of Easter eggs before the family heads off to Easter Mass in their Sunday best.

A Catholic child's baptism is often held two weeks after birth, on the first Sunday of the month. It is customary for the child's godparents to bring the child to church for the baptism, as the mother remains in confinement after the birth.

The child's first Holy Communion is another highly important occasion, usually taking place when a child turns eight. Exceptional care is taken when selecting the child's attire for this day and white is often the colour of preference as it is believed to symbolise purity. The girls wear a white dress and veil, while boys would be decked out in smart white shirts and trousers.

Unlike most of their Asian counterparts, Eurasians do not practise matchmaking in marital unions. In the past, it was tradition for the groom to propose marriage by approaching the bride's family, and in some instances, a formal letter would be presented.

The planning of the wedding would centre on the bride's family, with the reception usually held at her parents' home. Weddings were usually held on Saturday mornings, after which the guests would stay on for the wedding reception where snacks such as curry puffs, sausage rolls, cream puffs, sambal and ham sandwiches were served, with the highlight being the multi-tiered wedding cake. Wedding cakes were usually ordered from Cona's in Katong, G H Café in Battery Road or Victoria Confectionery (Ah Teng's) at Victoria Street. These bakeries were famed for their sugee wedding cakes, made from a delicious mix of semolina, flour and ground almonds.

The wedding reception would feature a live band, sometimes comprising the wedding guests themselves, and the classic song played at weddings was the Jinkli (or Jingli) Nona, a traditional Portuguese Malaccan folk song. In line with their European heritage, Eurasians would send off the newly-weds with showers of confetti as they drove away in the wedding car, which would have cans and bottles tied to the bumper, creating a joyous clamour.

The Sunday following the wedding day is observed as a day of thanksgiving. The newly-weds would attend Mass and then pay visits to everyone involved in the wedding preparations. The newly-weds would then host a lunch where they would serve guests as a gesture of their appreciation.

Celebrating Life

Celebration and music have long been a part of the Eurasian identity and lifestyle. Their significance goes beyond mere fun and festivities—they are a means of fostering and strengthening a communal

Quentin's mother, Freda, leaving Kampong Serani with
her father on her wedding day, on 9 January 1965.

The wedding recessional of newly-weds Robin and Freda Pereira, 1965.

identity, a time to share news and gossip, a way of supporting each other morally and emotionally, and a mode of social networking.

Reflecting the fusion of diverse ethnic origins, popular dishes and snacks served at these celebrations included curry *debal* (page 154), agar-agar, *kueh dodol*, sugee cake and *blueda*, a Dutch-inspired cake with a local flavour of fermented coconut tree sap known as toddy, which was used as a raising agent.

More than any other ethnic groups in Singapore, Eurasians truly valued music in parties and celebrations. Live bands were common and often comprised family members and friends. Dancing went with the music, and a popular dance was the *branyo*, a combination of Portuguese folk dance and the Malay *ronggeng*. European styles of dance such as the waltz, foxtrot and ballroom were also popular. This tradition still continues today along with contemporary dance styles.

During the pre-war and post-war years, Eurasians living in communal areas often held open house fetes where they were never short on guests. Such events were also held in the SRC, Victoria Memorial Hall and the Girls' Sports Club. Bringing in the New Year continues to be a major social celebration among the Eurasians today.

While there is no longer a distinct Eurasian enclave in Singapore, a majority of Eurasian families still live in the Katong and East Coast areas. The Eurasian Association (EA) which was formed in 1919 to serve the community, continues to engage its members through projects and programmes to promote the economic, social, cultural, physical and intellectual advancement of the Eurasians in Singapore.

A New Year's Eve dance organised by the Singapore Girls' Sports Club, circa 1950.

BASIC RECIPES

SAMBAL BELACAN

Makes about 200 g (7 oz)

Dried prawn (shrimp) paste (*belacan*) 2 Tbsp
Red chillies 12, stems removed
Red bird's eye chillies 5, stems removed
Kaffir lime leaf 1
Limes 4

1. Roast prawn paste by pan-frying without any oil, flipping it constantly to roast all sides, until it starts to break up and become powdery. Set aside.

2. Break red chillies into smaller pieces and remove seeds.

3. Pound or grind red chillies together with bird's eye chillies, kaffir lime leaf and roasted prawn paste into a rough paste.

4. If not using immediately, spoon paste into an airtight container and store refrigerated.

5. To serve as a condiment, spoon some into a saucer and drizzle with lime juice.

NOTE

- The Eurasians typically serve this spicy dried prawn and chilli paste as a condiment with every meal, even if the dishes are already spicy. Besides using it as a condiment, it is also used as a base in various dishes.

CHILI CHUKA

Makes about 250 g (9 oz)

Red chillies 12, stems removed

Red bird's eye chillies 5, stems removed

Garlic 6 cloves, peeled

Ginger 3-cm (1^1/$_4$-in) knob, peeled

White vinegar 6 Tbsp

Light soy sauce ^{1}/$_2$ Tbsp

Sugar 1 Tbsp

1. Break red chillies into smaller pieces and remove seeds.

2. Pound or grind red chillies together with bird's eye chillies, garlic, ginger, vinegar, soy sauce and sugar until smooth.

3. Taste and adjust with more vinegar if desired. Serve or store refrigerated in an airtight container.

NOTE

- This condiment is used for dips. There are many versions, but this is my favourite. It is easy to do and gives a good kick to dishes it is served with.

APPETISERS & STARTERS

ACAR TIMUN SERANI

Makes 600 g (1 lb 5¹/₃ oz)

This Eurasian style cucumber pickle can be served as a salad or side dish. To serve it as a salad, all you need to do is to toss it with some shredded lettuce leaves. It makes a refreshing side dish served with curries.

Dried prawns (shrimps) 100 g (3¹/₂ oz)

Cucumbers 3

Green chillies 2

Onions 2, peeled and thinly sliced

White vinegar 1 Tbsp

Sugar 6 Tbsp

Light soy sauce 2 Tbsp

Sambal *belacan* (page 30) 2 Tbsp

1. Rinse and soak dried prawns for 5 minutes, then drain and pat-dry with paper towels. Pound or grind prawns into floss. Transfer to a bowl and set aside.

2. Peel cucumbers and cut lengthwise into quarters. Remove soft centres. Slice on the diagonal. Set aside.

3. Wash green chillies and remove stems. Slice on the diagonal and remove seeds.

4. Place cucumbers, chillies and onions in a bowl with prawn floss. Add vinegar, sugar, soy sauce and sambal *belacan* and mix well.

5. Refrigerate for about 30 minutes. Serve chilled.

SAMBAL ACAR NANAS

Makes 500 g (1 lb 1½ oz)

This sweet, spicy and refreshing pineapple pickle is a must-have when serving a noodle dish known as Birthday *mee* (page 152), much like *kerabu timun nanas* which the Peranakans typically serve with Nonya *mee*.

Ripe pineapple 1, medium

Cucumber 1

Sugar 3 Tbsp

White vinegar 1 Tbsp

Light soy sauce 2 Tbsp

Sambal *belacan* (page 30) 4 Tbsp

1. Cut stem off pineapple, then trim off skin and eyes. Cut pineapple into wedges, then slice off core. Cut wedges into narrower strips, then chop finely. Place into a large bowl.

2. Peel cucumbers and cut lengthwise into quarters. Remove soft centres and chop finely. Add to bowl with pineapple.

3. Add sugar, vinegar, soy sauce and sambal *belacan* to bowl and toss well until sugar is dissolved. Transfer to a plate and serve.

NOTE

· This dish can be made a day ahead and kept refrigerated until needed.

GREEN CHILLI SAMBAL

Serves 6–8

An elderly Eurasian lady, Mrs Lena Fox, gave this recipe to me many years ago. This dish is somewhat similar to prawn *bostador* (page 160) in its use of green chillies, but here, the chillies are stuffed with fish paste, much like *yong tau foo,* a Hakka dish found at many hawker centres and food courts in Singapore today.

Green chillies 14, large

Cooking oil 3 Tbsp

Water 1 Tbsp

Sugar 1/2 Tbsp

Salt 1/4 Tbsp

Chicken stock cube 1

Coconut milk 100 ml (3 1/2 fl oz)

Limes 5, juice extracted

Fish Mixture

Fish fillet (any type of fish is fine) 300 g (11 oz), cut into small scraps

Light soy sauce 1 Tbsp

Ground white pepper 1/4 Tbsp

Cornflour (cornstarch) 1/4 Tbsp

Salt 1/4 Tbsp

Spice Paste

Shallots 20, peeled

Garlic 5 cloves, peeled

Candlenuts 3

Dried prawn (shrimp) paste (*belacan***)** 20 g (2/3 oz)

Turmeric 4-cm (1 1/2-in) knob, peeled and sliced

Dried chillies 20, cut into sections and soaked for 10 minutes

1. Combine ingredients for fish mixture and mix thoroughly.

2. Slit green chillies lengthwise but do not cut through. Remove seeds. Stuff chillies with fish mixture and set aside.

3. Pound or grind together ingredients for spice paste until fine.

4. Heat oil in a wok and fry spice paste until oil rises to the surface. Add water, sugar, salt and chicken stock cube. Add coconut milk gradually, stirring to mix.

5. Add stuffed green chillies to wok and simmer for 2 minutes. Add lime juice and remove from heat.

NOTE

- When choosing green chillies for this dish, pick the largest ones you can find as they will be easier to stuff.

CUCUMBER SALAD

Serves 6-8

I remember this to be one of the first salads I have ever tried. It may be a simple dish, but it is a comfort food for many Eurasians and it brings back many fond memories of childhood when it was a staple at every party. I have adapted the dish by dressing it with my own recipe for vinaigrette oil.

Salad

Cucumbers 2, medium

Local salad leaves 250 g (9 oz)

Large onion 1, peeled and thinly sliced, rings separated

Tomatoes 2, medium, sliced into rounds

Hard-boiled eggs 2, peeled and sliced across into rounds

Vinaigrette Oil Dressing

English parsley 2 sprigs

Coriander leaves (cilantro) 3 sprigs

Chili chuka (page 31) 6 Tbsp

Olive oil 6 Tbsp

White vinegar 2 Tbsp

Black peppercorns $1/4$ Tbsp, coarsely ground

1. Peel cucumbers, then use a fork to scrape cucumbers lengthwise to make long lines on the surface. Slice into thin rounds.

2. Place salad leaves on a large serving plate, then top with cucumbers, onion, tomatoes and eggs.

3. Prepare dressing. Chop parsley and coriander together finely.

4. Mix *chili chuka*, olive oil, vinegar and pepper in a bowl. Add parsley and coriander and mix well.

5. Pour dressing over salad just before serving.

NOTE

- When boiling the eggs, add 2 Tbsp oil and 1 Tbsp salt to the water. This will make the eggs easier to peel.

MEATY CUTLET

Makes 8 large cutlets

This is the Eurasian version of croquettes. It is great served as a starter or a complement to stews or curries with rice. Meaty cutlets are traditionally shaped large, but you can form smaller cutlets or shape them differently, if preferred.

Potatoes 4, large, boiled and peeled
Cooking oil as needed
Shallots 5, peeled and finely sliced
Spring onions (scallions) 50 g (1²/₃ oz)
Coriander leaves (cilantro) 50 g (1²/₃ oz)
Corned beef 340 g (12 oz)
Eggs 2, beaten
Breadcrumbs 300 g (11 oz)
Onion 1, peeled and sliced

1. Boil a pot of water and cook potatoes until tender. Drain potatoes and leave to cool before peeling.
2. Heat some oil in a wok over medium heat. Add shallots and fry until lightly browned. Remove and set aside to drain.
3. Chop spring onions and coriander together finely.
4. Place peeled potatoes in a bowl with corned beef and mash together. Add spring onions, coriander and fried shallots. Mix well.
5. Divide mixture into 8 portions. Shape with hands into balls.
6. Heat oil for deep-frying. Place beaten egg and breadcrumbs into separate shallow dishes.
7. Dip a meat cutlet into beaten egg and then into breadcrumbs and lower it gently into hot oil. Lower heat and cook until cutlet is golden brown. Remove and set aside to drain. Repeat until all cutlets are cooked.
8. Serve hot, garnished with sliced onions.

NOTE

· The oil has to be very hot when the cutlets are added to ensure that a crisp outer coating forms around the cutlets. Lower the heat when the cutlets are frying to prevent them from browning too much while cooking.

CALAMARI FRITTERS

Serves 4-6

The batter for this recipe is light and crisp, and can be used not just for coating calamari but also for prawns (shrimps) and fish fillets. Calamari fritters are best served freshly cooked, so prepare them just before serving. This dish can be served with other side dishes as a meal, or as a snack to go with drinks.

Squid (calamari) 1 kg (2 lb 3 oz)

Cooking oil 500 ml (16 fl oz / 2 cups)

Batter

Plain (all-purpose) flour 3 Tbsp

Rice flour 3 Tbsp

Cornflour (cornstarch) 1 Tbsp

Salt 1 Tbsp

Ground white pepper 1 Tbsp

Light soy sauce 1 Tbsp

Beer 100 ml ($3^1/_2$ fl oz)

Eggs 2

1. To clean squid, firmly pull head and body tube apart. The head and innards should slip out of the body. Trim off innards by cutting below the eyes. Discard. Squeeze between the eyes to remove the beak (which is located at the base of the tentacles) and discard. Remove cartilage from inside body and discard. Rinse squid and cut into rings about 1-cm ($^1/_2$-in) thick. Set aside.

2. Prepare batter. Combine plain and rice flours, salt and pepper in a bowl. Add soy sauce and beer, followed by eggs. Mix well to obtain a smooth and thick batter.

3. Place squid into batter and coat well.

4. Heat oil in a wok and gently lower squid one piece at a time into hot oil.

5. Cook until golden brown. Remove from oil and drain well. Serve with *chili chuka* (page 31)

DEVIL WINGS

This dish of fried chicken wings has a fiery-hot aftertaste. The heat can be moderated by adjusting the quantity of dried chillies and chilli powder added to the spice paste. To really spice it up however, bird's eye chillies can be added to the spice paste. Serve as part of a meal or as a snack with drinks.

Chicken wings 1 kg (2 lb 3 oz) or about 10 medium wings, washed and drained

Cooking oil 500 ml (16 fl oz / 2 cups)

Batter

Plain (all-purpose) flour 3 Tbsp

Rice flour 3 Tbsp

Chilli powder $1/2$ Tbsp

Salt $1/2$ Tbsp

Ground black pepper 1 Tbsp

Light soy sauce 1 Tbsp

Water 200 ml (7 fl oz)

Eggs 2

Spice Paste

Shallots 50 g ($1^2/3$ oz), peeled and chopped

Large onion 50 g ($1^2/3$ oz), peeled and chopped

Ginger 50 g ($1^2/3$ oz), peeled and sliced

Red chillies 50 g ($1^2/3$ oz), stalks removed

Dried chillies 20 g ($2/3$ oz), cut into sections and soaked for 10 minutes, seeds removed

Mustard seeds 5 g ($1/5$ oz)

Chilli powder 30 g (1 oz)

1. Pound or grind together ingredients for spice paste until fine. Rub paste over chicken wings and leave to marinate for at least 30 minutes.

2. Prepare batter. Combine plain and rice flours, chilli powder, salt and pepper in a bowl. Add soy sauce and water, then eggs and mix well to obtain a smooth batter.

3. Add marinated chicken wings to batter and coat well.

4. Heat oil in a wok over medium heat. When oil is hot, gently lower chicken wings in one at a time. Cook in small batches. Chicken wings are cooked when they start floating to the surface.

5. Remove from oil and drain well before serving.

NOTE

· When frying chicken wings, ensure that the oil is moderately hot, so the chicken will be cooked through without being burnt. Test by dropping some batter into the oil. It should turn golden brown and float gradually.

SEYBAK

Serves 8–10

This salad of braised pork is traditionally made with pig's ears, which lends a lovely crunchy texture to the dish. It can be omitted and replaced with more pork belly if preferred. This dish is great as an appetiser and it goes well with beer.

Pork belly 1 kg (2 lb 3 oz), cut into chunks

Pig's ears 300 g (11 oz), thoroughly cleaned

Cooking oil 4 Tbsp

Onion 1, peeled and sliced

Garlic 8 cloves, peeled and chopped

Cinnamon 2 sticks, each about 5-cm (2-in)

Cloves 5

Star anise 4

Cardamom 3 pods

Black peppercorns 10 g ($^1/_3$ oz)

Galangal 3-cm (1$^1/_4$-in) knob, peeled and thickly sliced

Dark soy sauce 2 Tbsp

Ground white pepper 1 Tbsp

Water 500 ml (16 fl oz / 2 cups)

Rock sugar 2 Tbsp

Marinade

Dark soy sauce 4 Tbsp

Light soy sauce 1 Tbsp

Ground white pepper 1 Tbsp

Salad

Cooking oil for deep-frying

Firm bean curd 4, each cut into quarters

Fried bean curd puffs 4, blanched and thinly sliced

Local salad leaves 300 g (11 oz), shredded

Cucumbers 2, medium, halved and thinly sliced

Tomatoes 2, medium, halved and thinly sliced

Onion 1, peeled and cut into thin rings

Chilli Sauce

Red chillies 7, stems removed

Garlic 8 cloves, peeled

Ginger 3-cm (1$^1/_4$-in) knob, peeled

Galangal 1 slice, about 0.5-cm ($^1/_4$-in) thick

Light soy sauce 1 Tbsp

White vinegar 4 Tbsp

Sugar 1$^1/_2$ Tbsp

Lime juice 1 Tbsp

1. Combine ingredients for marinade in a bowl. Add pork belly and pig's ears and leave to marinate while preparing rest of ingredients.

2. Heat oil in a pot and add onion, garlic, cinnamon, cloves, star anise, cardamom, peppercorns and galangal. When onion starts to brown, add marinated pork and pig's ears, soy sauces and pepper.

3. Stir-fry pork for 3 minutes, then add water and boil until pork is tender and gravy is thickened. Add rock sugar and remove from heat when rock sugar has dissolved.

4. Leave to cool before slicing meat into bite-size pieces.

5. Prepare salad. Heat oil for deep-frying and deep-fry firm bean curd until lightly brown. Remove from heat and drain well.

6. Combine ingredients for salad in a bowl.

7. Pound or grind together ingredients for chilli sauce. Transfer to a bowl.

8. To serve, place salad ingredients on a plate, arranging firm bean curd on top. Add sliced pork and ears and drizzle with chilli sauce.

NOTE

· If using pig's ears, be sure to clean them properly and remove any hair. To do this, use a disposable shaver or a blow torch.

SOUPS & VEGETABLES

TIM SOUP

Serves 6-8

This soup made from black beans and pork bones is traditionally prepared on New Year's Day within the Eurasian community. I have always enjoyed having this soup for lunch on the first day of the year for as long as I can remember. The Peranakans also have a similar soup in their repertoire, but their version of this dish is prepared using duck and is known as *itek tim*.

Cooking oil 2 Tbsp

Garlic 5 cloves, peeled and chopped

Pork ribs 500 g (1 lb 1¹/₂ oz)

Light soy sauce 2 Tbsp

Chicken stock cubes 2

Ground white pepper 1 Tbsp

Sour plums 2

Black beans 200 g (7 oz), soaked in hot water for 1 hour, then skinned

Water 1.5 litres (48 fl oz / 6 cups)

Salted vegetable (*kiam chye*) 200 g (7 oz), cut into bite-size pieces

Tomatoes 2, cut into quarters

Garnish

Spring onion (scallion) 1, cut into short lengths

Local celery 1 sprig, cut into short lengths

1. Heat oil in a pot and fry garlic and pork ribs until garlic starts to brown.

2. Add soy sauce, chicken stock cubes and pepper. Mix well and add sour plums, skinned black beans and water. Let soup simmer until pork is tender.

3. Add salted vegetable and tomatoes and allow soup to return to the boil. When soup starts to boil, remove from heat.

4. Serve hot, garnished with spring onion and coriander.

NOTE

• If desired, 2 whole garlic bulbs can be added to the soup together with the pork bones. When the garlic bulbs start to soften, it is an indicator that the pork is almost ready.

PRAWN BALL SOUP

Serves 4-6

This soup is clearly a Chinese influence and the Peranakans also have a similar but more elaborate dish known as *pong tauhu*. This prawn ball soup is easy to make and very tasty. The prawn balls go very well with a dip of *chili chuka* (page 31).

Cooking oil 2 Tbsp	**Prawn Balls**
Garlic 5 cloves, peeled and chopped	**Prawns (shrimps)** 500 g (1 lb 1½ oz)
Light soy sauce 2 Tbsp	**Silken bean curd** 225 g (8 oz)
Chicken stock cubes 2	**Spring onion (scallion)** 1, finely chopped
Ground white pepper 1 Tbsp	**Coriander leaves (cilantro)** 1 sprig, finely chopped
Water 1.5 litres (48 fl oz / 6 cups)	**Ground white pepper** ½ Tbsp
Cabbage leaves 300 g (11 oz), sliced	**Cornflour (cornstarch)** ½ Tbsp
Coriander leaves (cilantro) 1 sprig, cut into short sections	**Light soy sauce** ½ Tbsp

1. Prepare prawn balls. Peel prawns and remove heads. Slit prawns along the back and remove the black intestine. Rinse well and pat dry. Dice prawns with a cleaver, then use repeated chopping motions to mince them coarsely on the chopping board. Place in a bowl.

2. Add bean curd to prawns and mash together. Add spring onion, coriander, pepper, cornflour and soy sauce. Mix well and set aside.

3. Heat oil in a saucepan and fry garlic until it starts to brown. Add soy sauce, chicken stock cubes, pepper and water and bring to the boil.

4. When soup is boiling, make prawn balls. Using 2 tablespoons, shape prawn mixture into 2.5-cm (1-in) balls and add to boiling soup.

5. Add cabbage and let it cook for about 2 minutes before removing from heat. Dish out and garnish with coriander. Serve hot.

MULLIGATAWNY

Serves 6-8

As a child, I remember this soup being served for supper after midnight Mass every Christmas Eve. The extended family would gather at my parents' home and we would have a feast. This soup somehow made the occasion extra special for me. A spicy Indian chicken soup, mulligatawny tastes like curry but is watery like soup.

Cooking oil 2 Tbsp

Finely chopped ginger 1 Tbsp

Finely chopped garlic 1 Tbsp

Onion 1, peeled and finely sliced

Bay leaves 2

Chickpea flour 3 Tbsp

Meat curry powder 2 Tbsp

Ground turmeric $1/4$ Tbsp

Ground white pepper 1 Tbsp

Light soy sauce 2 Tbsp

Chicken stock cubes 2

Green apple 1, skinned, cored and cubed

Tomatoes 2, chopped

Water 1 litre (32 fl oz / 4 cups)

Boneless chicken breast 300 g (11 oz)

Garnishing

Spring onion (scallion) 1, chopped

Coriander leaves (cilantro) 1 sprig, chopped

1. Heat oil in a pan and add ginger, garlic and onion. Stir-fry until garlic starts to brown.

2. Add bay leaves, chickpea flour, meat curry powder, turmeric, pepper, soy sauce, chicken stock cubes, green apple and tomatoes. Mix well and add water.

3. Let soup simmer, then add chicken. Cover pot with a lid and cook for 15 minutes.

4. Remove chicken from pot and leave to cool slightly before shredding.

5. Leave soup to boil until apple starts to soften. Return shredded chicken to pot and boil for another 5 minutes before removing from heat.

6. Dish out and garnish with spring onion and coriander. Serve hot.

NOTE

· To help the chicken cool more quickly for shredding, place it into a bowl of cold water for 10 minutes. Drain well before shredding.

CALDU PESCADOR

Serves 6-8

Also known as fisherman's soup, this dish is so-named because it was first prepared by fishermen using a variety of seafood from their day's catch. It is a simple dish that will help whet the appetite. You can vary the seafood used according to taste. This soup is best enjoyed hot and can be served with rice or bread.

Water 1.5 litres (48 fl oz / 6 cups)

Onion 1, peeled and quartered

Garlic 3 cloves, peeled

Lemon grass 2 stalks, hard outer leaves removed, ends trimmed and bruised

Kaffir lime leaves 4, crushed

Dried sour fruit 1 slice

Red bird's eye chillies 4

Salt $^1/_2$ Tbsp

Ground white pepper $^1/_2$ Tbsp

Sugar $^1/_2$ Tbsp

Light soy sauce 2 Tbsp

Coriander leaves (cilantro) 1 sprig, finely chopped

Seafood

Mussels 400 g (14$^1/_3$ oz)

Prawns (shrimps) 300 g (11 oz)

Squid 200 g (7 oz)

Fish fillet 200 g (7 oz)

Crab meat 100 g (3$^1/_2$ oz)

1. Scrub mussels to remove any dirt on shells. Discard any that are open or have shells that are chipped. Soak in a large basin of water for about 20 minutes to allow mussels to expel any sand. Lift mussels out of the water, being careful not to agitate the sand collected at the base of basin. Repeat to soak the mussels a second time. Pull beards off just before cooking.

2. Peel prawns and remove heads, leaving tails intact. Slit prawns along the back and remove the black intestine. Rinse well and pat dry.

3. To clean squid, firmly pull head and body tube apart. The head and innards should slip out of the body. Trim off innards by cutting below the eyes. Discard. Squeeze between the eyes to remove the beak (which is located at the base of the tentacles) and discard. Remove cartilage from inside body and discard. Rinse squid and cut into rings about 1-cm ($^1/_2$-in) thick.

4. Bring water to the boil in a pot. Add onion, garlic, lemon grass and kaffir lime leaves, followed by mussels, prawns, squid, fish and crab meat. Simmer for 1 minute, until prawns change colour.

5. Add dried sour fruit and bird's eye chillies. Season with salt, pepper, sugar and soy sauce. Remove from heat.

6. Dish out and garnish with coriander. Serve hot.

NOTE

· Bruising the lemon grass before cooking ensures that its fragrance is released. Do this by bending it with your hands. Do the same with the kaffir leaves by crushing them with your hands before adding to the pot.

PICE

Serves 4-6

This spicy dish is unique as wolf herring is first marinated with chilli paste, then wrapped with Chinese cabbage leaves and boiled in the soup. My dad used to fry pork lard and add it to this soup as a crispy and flavourful garnish. *Patah* chilli is a simple condiment made with lime juice, soy sauce and chillies, and it goes well as a dip for the fish parcels.

Wolf herring (*ikan parang*) 6 fillets, each about 100 g (3¹/₂ oz), washed and cleaned

Green Chinese cabbage 1 kg (2 lb 3 oz), leaves separated

Cooking oil 2 Tbsp

Water 1 litre (32 fl oz / 4 cups)

Light soy sauce 2 Tbsp

Chicken stock cube 1

Chilli Paste

Dried chillies 100 g (3¹/₂ oz), cut into short sections and soaked for 10 minutes, seeds removed

Candlenuts 2

Salt ¹/₂ tsp

Patah Chilli

Limes 2, juice extracted

Dark soy sauce 6 Tbsp

Red chillies 2

1. Prepare chilli paste. Pound or grind dried chillies together with candlenuts and salt into a paste.

2. Rub each piece of fish with 1 Tbsp chilli paste and leave for 10 minutes. Set remaining chilli paste aside.

3. Wrap each piece of fish with 2–3 cabbage leaves and set aside. Slice remaining cabbage leaves into smaller pieces.

4. Prepare *patah* chilli. Mix lime juice and soy sauce in a small bowl, then break chillies into bowl. Set aside.

5. Heat oil in a wok. Add chilli paste and fry until oil rises. Add water, soy sauce and chicken stock cube and bring to the boil. Add fish parcels and cabbage leaves.

6. Simmer over low heat for 15 minutes until cabbage is tender and fish is cooked. Remove from heat.

7. Dish out and garnish with deep-fried pork lard if desired. Serve hot with *patah* chilli on the side.

NOTE

- Scalding the cabbage leaves with hot water will soften them and make wrapping the fish easier.

STIR-FRIED KANGKONG

Serves 4–6

Many Asian cuisines have recipes for *kangkong* or water spinach, a popular dish being a stir-fry prepared with sambal *belacan* and dried prawns (shrimps). The Eurasian take on this stir-fry is lighter in flavour, accompanied only with onion, garlic, red chilli and tomato. This simple dish goes well with rice.

Water spinach (*kangkong*) 1 kg (2 lb 3 oz)
Cooking oil 4 Tbsp
Onion 1, peeled and sliced
Red chilli 1, stem removed and sliced
Tomato 1, sliced
Garlic 3 cloves, peeled and sliced
Salt ¼ Tbsp
Light soy sauce 1 Tbsp

1. Trim off lower stems of water spinach and discard. Pluck leaves and cut stems into short lengths. Rinse well.
2. Heat oil in a wok and fry onion, chilli, tomato and garlic until onion is soft.
3. Add salt, soy sauce and water spinach. Fry for about 1 minute, mixing thoroughly. Dish out and serve hot.

NOTE

• Increase the number of chillies added if a spicier dish is preferred.

CHAP CHYE

Serves 4-6

Chap chye is the Hokkien term for mixed vegetables. It is a signature dish of the Peranakans, but the other ethnic groups in Singapore also have their own versions of this dish. This is the Eurasian version of *chap chye*. Serve it as part of a meal with other dishes and white rice.

Garlic 6 cloves, peeled

Preserved soy bean paste (*taucheo*) 3 Tbsp

Cooking oil 3 Tbsp

Ground white pepper 1 Tbsp

Light soy sauce 1 Tbsp

Salt 1/2 Tbsp

Water 3 Tbsp

Dried Chinese mushrooms 5, soaked to soften, stems discarded and sliced

Dried black fungus 4, soaked to soften, hard parts trimmed and discarded, then sliced

Dried lily buds 50 g (1²/₃ oz), soaked to soften and knotted

Yam bean 1, peeled and sliced

Carrot 1, peeled and sliced

Canned button mushrooms 250 g (9 oz), drained and cut into quarters

Onions 2, peeled and cut into quarters

Glass vermicelli (*tanghoon*) 50 g (1²/₃ oz), soaked to soften

Cabbage leaves 300 g (11 oz), cut into bite-size pieces

Celery 1 stalk, sliced

Firm bean curd 2 pieces, cut into cubes and deep-fried

Bean curd sticks 100 g (3¹/₂ oz)

Spring onions (scallions) 50 g (1²/₃ oz), cut into 8-cm (3-in) lengths

Local celery 50 g (1²/₃ oz), cut into short lengths

1. Pound or grind together garlic and preserved soy bean paste until fine.

2. Heat oil in a wok and fry paste until fragrant. Add pepper, soy sauce, salt and water, then add mushrooms, fungus, lily buds, yam bean, carrot, button mushrooms and onions. Fry for 2 minutes.

3. Add glass vermicelli, cabbage, celery and fried firm bean curd. Cover wok with a lid and leave to cook for 3 minutes.

4. Break bean curd sticks into wok and mix thoroughly.

5. Dish out and serve hot, garnished with spring onions and local celery.

NOTE

• The lily buds are typically knotted before cooking to avoid them breaking up when cooking.

AUBERGINE PATCHRI

Serves 4-6

Patchri is a sweet, sour and spicy sauce. There are recipes for pineapple patchri, made famous in Goa. This is the Eurasian version, prepared with aubergines (eggplants/brinjals). This dish goes well with white rice.

Long purple aubergines
(eggplants/brinjals) 2

Ground white pepper 1 Tbsp

Salt 1 tsp

Cooking oil 2 Tbsp

Dill as desired

Patchri Sauce

Cooking oil 2 Tbsp

Shallots 5, peeled and sliced

Garlic 5 cloves, peeled and sliced

Ginger 5-cm (2-in) knob, peeled and sliced

Green chilli 1, stem removed and sliced

Red chilli 1, stem removed and sliced

Chilli powder 1 Tbsp

Ground turmeric $1/2$ Tbsp

Sugar 1 Tbsp

Tamarind pulp 1 Tbsp, mixed with
3 Tbsp water and strained

Salt to taste

1. Trim ends of aubergines, then slice lengthwise in half. Make cuts on the inside of the pieces, then rub with pepper and salt.

2. Heat oil in wok and fry aubergines until golden brown. Remove to a serving dish and set aside.

3. Prepare sauce. Heat oil in a wok and fry shallots, garlic, ginger and chillies until shallots are soft. Add chilli powder, ground turmeric, sugar, tamarind liquid and salt. Mix well. The sauce should be thick.

4. Spoon sauce over fried aubergines. Garnish with dill, if desired, and serve.

NOTE

· The sauce can be prepared in advance, but the aubergines are best fried just before serving.

FRIED AUBERGINES

Serves 4-6

This is another popular Eurasian dish prepared using aubergines. The oyster sauce is a Chinese influence and the chilli powder adds a touch of spiciness. It is a dish with a difference and I am sure those who enjoy eating aubergines would appreciate this dish. Serve it as part of a meal with rice.

Long purple aubergines
  (eggplants/brinjals) 2
Cooking oil 4 Tbsp
Garlic 5 cloves, peeled and chopped
Oyster sauce 3 Tbsp
Chilli powder 1 Tbsp
Ground white pepper $1/2$ Tbsp
Light soy sauce 1 Tbsp
Water 4 Tbsp
Chives 50 g ($1^2/_3$ fl oz), cut into
  5-cm (2-in) strips
Red chilli 1, sliced lengthwise,
  seeds removed

1. Trim ends of aubergines, then cut into 4 equal logs. Cut each log lengthwise into quarters.

2. Heat oil in a wok and fry garlic until it starts to brown. Add oyster sauce, chilli powder, pepper and soy sauce and mix well.

3. Add aubergines and water and mix well. Lower heat and cook covered for 3 minutes.

4. Arrange chives on a serving plate and dish aubergines out onto chives. Garnish with sliced chilli. Serve immediately.

NOTE

· Increase the amount of chilli powder added for a spicier dish.

FRIED LADIES' FINGERS

Serves 6-8

This dish originated from Goa. When fried this way, the ladies' fingers are not slimy but crunchy and flavourful. Use young ladies' fingers for this dish as they are more tender and less fibrous. Test by bending the tip of the ladies' finger. It should break off.

Cooking oil 5 Tbsp

Curry leaves 2 stalks, plucked

Dried chillies 4, cut and seeds removed

Onions 2, peeled and sliced

Mustard seeds 1 Tbsp

Garlic 5 cloves, peeled and chopped

Ladies' fingers 800 g ($1^3/_4$ lb),
    cut into 2-cm ($^3/_4$-in) lengths

Ground turmeric $^1/_2$ Tbsp

Salt $^1/_2$ Tbsp

1. Heat oil in a wok and add curry leaves, dried chillies, onions and mustard seeds. As curry leaves start to crisp, add chopped garlic and ladies' fingers. Lower heat and stir-fry to mix, then cover wok with a lid.

2. After 3 minutes, remove lid and add ground turmeric and salt. Stir-fry for about 1 minute, then remove from heat.

3. Dish out and serve hot.

MASAK LODEH SERANI

Serves 4-6

Lodeh is a mild vegetable and coconut milk curry. It has its origins in Java, Indonesia, where it is made using young jackfruit and aubergines. This is the Eurasian version of the dish, which is prepared using cabbage, carrot, yam bean and long beans. This is a versatile dish and you may choose to add or omit vegetables according to taste.

Cooking oil 4 Tbsp

Light soy sauce 1 Tbsp

Water 500 ml (16 fl oz / 2 cups)

Kaffir lime leaves 2

Cabbage $^1/_2$ medium head, cut into pieces 3-cm (1$^1/_4$-in) wide

Carrot 1, peeled and sliced

Yam bean 1, peeled and sliced

Long beans 6, cut into 5-cm (2-in) lengths

Coconut milk 300 ml (10 fl oz / 1$^1/_4$ cups)

Salt $^1/_2$ Tbsp

Chilli Paste

Dried prawns (shrimps) 100 g (3$^1/_2$ oz)

Large onions 2, peeled and sliced

Dried chillies 15, cut into short lengths, soaked for 10 minutes, seeds removed

Dried prawn (shrimp) paste (*belacan*) 50 g (1$^2/_3$ oz)

Turmeric 10-cm (4-in) knob, peeled

Lemon grass 2 stalks, ends trimmed, tough outer leaves removed and sliced

1. Pound or grind ingredients for chilli paste until fine.

2. Heat oil in a pot and fry chilli paste until fragrant. Add soy sauce and fry for about 1 minute, then add water, kaffir lime leaves, cabbage, carrot, yam bean and long beans. Bring to boil.

3. Lower heat and add coconut milk and salt. Remove from heat. Dish out and serve hot.

NOTE

· Cut all the vegetables into pieces of the same length so that they will cook more evenly.

MEAT & POULTRY

DHALL KRISTANG

Serves 6-8

This mutton and lentil curry is very similar to the Indian dhal curries, except that the Indian curries are usually vegetarian. This Eurasian curry is also spicier and includes potatoes, carrots and eggs. Note that the eggs should be done like poached eggs. I enjoy eating this dish with rice and sambal *belacan* (page 30).

Cooking oil 4 Tbsp

Onions 2, peeled and sliced

Ginger 5 cm (2-in) knob, peeled and thickly sliced

Cinnamon sticks 2, each about 5-cm (2-in)

Cloves 10

Star anise 2

Cardamom 3 pods

White peppercorns 10

Dried chillies 5, halved, seeds removed

Mutton ribs 1 kg (2 lb 3 oz), cut into individual ribs

Chilli powder 2 Tbsp

Curry powder 2 Tbsp

Ground turmeric 1 Tbsp

Light soy sauce 2 Tbsp

Dhal 50 g ($1^2/_3$ oz), washed and soaked for at least 1 hour to soften

Water 1 litre (32 fl oz / 4 cups)

Carrot 1, peeled and cut into 2-cm ($^3/_4$-in) chunks

Potatoes 2, peeled and quartered

Eggs 4

1. Heat oil in a pot and fry onions, ginger, cinnamon sticks, cloves, star anise, cardamom, peppercorns and dried chillies until onions start to brown.

2. Add mutton and fry for 1 minute, then add chili powder, curry powder, ground turmeric and soy sauce. Mix and cook for another 5 minutes more.

3. Add dhal and water and boil for 15 minutes.

4. Add carrots and potatoes, then lower heat and cook until carrots and potatoes are soft.

5. Break eggs into pot. Do not stir as the eggs should be whole. Remove from heat.

6. Dish out and serve hot.

NOTE

- Ensure that the eggs are poached and not overcooked. Once they change from translucent to white, remove from heat.
- To avoid dropping any egg shell into the soup, crack eggs into a bowl before pouring into curry.

KRISTANG STEW

Serves 6–8

Made with chicken, vegetables and lots of gravy, this stew can be served as a meal on its own. Though stews typically spot a thick gravy, this stew is probably influenced by the Chinese and has a thin gravy, but it is nevertheless very flavourful. This stew can be served with rice or bread and sambal *belacan* (page 30) on the side.

Chicken 1, about 1.5 kg (3 lb 4¹/₂ oz), cut into smaller pieces

Light soy sauce 4 Tbsp + 4 Tbsp

Ground white pepper 2 Tbsp

Cooking oil 4 Tbsp

Large onions 4, peeled; 3 sliced and 1 quartered

Cinnamon stick 1, about 5-cm (2-in)

Cloves 10

Star anise 2

Cardamom 3 pods

White peppercorns 10

Water 1 litre (32 fl oz / 4 cups)

Carrots 2, peeled and cubed

Potatoes 2, peeled and quartered

Cabbage ¹/₂ medium head, leaves separated

Coriander leaves (cilantro) 3 sprigs

1. Place chicken in a bowl with 4 Tbsp soy sauce and 2 Tbsp ground white pepper and leave to marinate for 20 minutes.

2. Heat oil in a pot and fry sliced onions, cinnamon, cloves, star anise, cardamom and peppercorns until onions start to brown.

3. Add marinated chicken and 4 Tbsp soy sauce. Fry chicken for about 1 minute, then add water, carrots and potatoes and cook until carrots and potatoes are soft.

4. Add cabbage and quartered onion and cook until cabbage is soft. Remove from heat.

5. Dish out and garnish with coriander. Serve hot.

NOTE

- Vary this dish by substituting chicken with beef or corned beef. Cocktail sausages can also be added to this stew.

FRIED PERMENTA CHICKEN

Serves 6–8

This stir-fried dish of chicken in pepper sauce is very versatile. The chicken can be substituted with beef, prawns (shrimps), fish fillet and even crabs. When cooking this dish with crabs, however, I prefer to omit the capsicums (bell peppers).

Boneless chicken 1 kg (2 lb 3 oz), cubed
Light soy sauce 3 Tbsp
Ground white pepper 2 Tbsp + 1 Tbsp
Cooking oil 1 Tbsp
Butter 3 Tbsp
Onion 1, peeled and sliced
Black peppercorns 2 Tbsp
Garlic 5 cloves, peeled and chopped
Water 100 ml (3^1/$_2$ fl oz)

Dark soy sauce 2 Tbsp
Salt ^{1}/$_4$ Tbsp
Red capsicum (bell pepper) 1, cored, seeded and sliced
Green capsicum (bell pepper) 1, cored, seeded and sliced
Cornflour (cornstarch) ^{1}/$_4$ Tbsp, mixed with 2 Tbsp water
Coriander leaves (cilantro) 1 sprig

1. Place chicken in a bowl with light soy sauce and 2 Tbsp ground white pepper and leave to marinate for 20 minutes.

2. Heat oil and butter in a pot and fry onion, peppercorns and garlic until garlic starts to brown.

3. Add marinated chicken and fry until chicken changes colour.

4. Add water, dark soy sauce, salt and 1 Tbsp pepper and fry until chicken is cooked through.

5. Add capsicums and stir in cornflour mixture to thicken sauce. Remove from heat.

6. Dish out and serve hot, garnished with coriander.

NOTE

- If you prefer to turn up the heat on this dish, add sliced bird's eye chilli to the pot.

CURRY SEKU

Serves 6-8

This dry curry got its name from the wok, or *seku*, as it is known in the Malaccan Portuguese patois, that the curry is cooked in. *Seku* means bottom and the wok was probably so-named because of the roundness of its shape that resembled the human bottom. Curry *seku* is a very dry curry, not unlike the Indian dry masala (*peretal*).

Cooking oil 4 Tbsp

Onion 1, peeled and sliced

Garlic 3 cloves, peeled and sliced

Ginger 3-cm (1^1/$_4$-in) knob, peeled and cut into thin strips

Curry leaves 1 stalk

Cinnamon 1 stick, about 5-cm (2-in)

Cloves 4

Star anise 1

Cardamom 1 pod

Light soy sauce 2 Tbsp

Curry powder 125 g (4^1/$_2$ oz)

Chilli powder 1 Tbsp

Chicken 1, about 1.5 kg (3 lb 4^1/$_2$ oz), cut into smaller pieces

Potatoes 2, peeled and cut into 2-cm (1^1/$_4$ -in) cubes

Water 100 ml (3^1/$_2$ fl oz)

Salt ^{1}/$_4$ Tbsp

Ground Paste

Large onions 5, peeled and sliced

Ginger 10-cm (4-in) knob, peeled and sliced

Garlic 15 cloves, peeled

Dried chillies 100 g (3^1/$_2$ oz), cut into short lengths, soaked for 10 minutes, seeds removed

1. Pound or grind together ingredients for ground paste until fine. Set aside.

2. Heat oil in a pot over medium heat and fry sliced onion, garlic, ginger and curry leaves until onion is soft.

3. Add cinnamon, cloves, star anise and cardamom, followed by ground ingredients. Fry until oil rises.

4. Add soy sauce, curry powder and chili powder. Mix thoroughly.

5. Add chicken, potatoes and water. Continue stirring until curry thickens, chicken is cooked and potatoes are tender. This may take about 10 minutes. Season with salt.

6. Remove from heat. Dish out and serve hot.

NOTE

· When frying to thicken the curry, stir continuously to avoid the curry burning at the bottom of the pot.

CURRY CAPTAIN

Serves 6-8

There are many versions of this curry and some recipes include Chinese sausages (*lap cheong*) or luncheon meat. This version is my dad's and it was what he used to cook for the family when we were growing up.

Cooking oil 4 Tbsp

Chicken 1, about 1.5 kg (3 lb 4^1/$_2$ oz), cut into bite-size pieces

Bacon bones 200 g (7 oz), cut into bite-size pieces

Dark soy sauce 1 Tbsp

Water 50 ml (1^2/$_3$ fl oz)

Onion 1, peeled and quartered

Salt ^{1}/$_2$ Tbsp

Sugar ^{1}/$_2$ Tbsp

Lemon juice 2 tsp

Chilli Paste

Shallots 15, peeled

Red chillies 8, stems removed

1. Pound or grind together ingredients for chilli paste until fine.
2. Heat oil a pot and fry chilli paste until fragrant.
3. Add chicken and bacon bones, then dark soy sauce and water. Mix well.
4. Lower heat and simmer until chicken is cooked. Add onion, salt, sugar and lemon juice. Remove from heat.
5. Dish out and serve hot.

CHICKEN MOERU CURRY

Serves 6–8

This dish is the Eurasian version of Indian chicken curry. It is full of flavour from the variety of aromatics and spices used. If desired, the chicken can be substituted with beef or mutton. To keep the cooking time short, cut the beef or mutton into small cubes. This spicy dish goes well with rice.

Cooking oil 4 Tbsp

Onion 1, peeled and sliced

Garlic 20 g ($^2/_3$ oz), peeled and sliced

Ginger 20 g ($^2/_3$ oz), peeled and sliced

Cinnamon 1 stick, about 5-cm (2-in)

Cloves 8

Star anise 2

Cardamom 3 pods

Curry leaves 1 stalk

Curry powder 125 g ($4^1/_2$ oz)

Chilli powder 2 Tbsp

Light soy sauce 2 Tbsp

Chicken 1, about 1.5 kg (3 lb $4^1/_2$ oz), cut into 16 pieces

Potatoes 2, peeled and quartered

Water 400 ml ($13^1/_3$ fl oz)

Salt $^1/_2$ Tbsp

Ground Paste

Large onions 8, peeled and sliced

Ginger 10-cm (4-in) knob, peeled and sliced

Garlic 15 cloves, peeled

Dried chillies 100 g ($3^1/_2$ oz), cut and soaked for 10 minutes, seeds removed

1. Pound or grind together ingredients for ground paste until fine. Set aside.

2. Heat oil in pot over low heat and fry onion, garlic, ginger, cinnamon, cloves, star anise, cardamom and curry leaves until onion is soft.

3. Add ground paste and fry until oil rises.

4. Add curry powder, chili powder and soy sauce. Mix thoroughly.

5. Add chicken, potatoes and water and simmer over low heat until chicken is cooked and potatoes are soft. This may take about 10 minutes. Season with salt.

6. Remove from heat. Serve hot.

NOTE

· When frying the spices in step 2, keep the heat low to prevent the spices from exploding in the pot.

MEAT & POULTRY 91

VINDALOO

Serves 6-8

This spicy curry can be prepared with chicken, beef, mutton or pork. Traditionally, it is prepared with pork as the pork will render its fat, adding to the flavour of the curry. A spicy and sour curry, vindaloo is best served with rice and a side dish of sambal *acar nanas* (page 36).

Cooking oil 4 Tbsp

Onion 1, peeled and sliced

Garlic 20 g (²/₃ oz), peeled and sliced

Ginger 20 g (²/₃ oz), peeled and sliced

Pork shoulder 1 kg (2 lb 3 oz), cubed

Light soy sauce 2 Tbsp

Potatoes 2, peeled and quartered

Water 200 ml (7 fl oz)

Salt ¹/₂ Tbsp

White vinegar 4 Tbsp

Ground Paste

Large onions 2, peeled and sliced

Ginger 10-cm (4-in) knob, peeled

Garlic 15 cloves, peeled

Dried chillies 100 g (3¹/₂ oz), cut into short lengths, soaked for 10 minutes, seeds removed

Spices

Cumin seeds 4 Tbsp

Mustard seeds 4 Tbsp

Black peppercorns 1 Tbsp

Cinnamon 1 stick, about 5-cm (2-in)

Cloves 4

Star anise 1

Cardamom 2 pods

1. Pound or grind together ingredients for ground paste until fine. Set aside.

2. Using a spice mill, grind spices into a fine powder. Set aside.

3. Heat oil in pot over low heat and fry sliced onion, garlic and ginger until onion is soft.

4. Add ground paste and ground spices and fry until oil rises.

5. Add pork and soy sauce and mix thoroughly.

6. Add potatoes and water and simmer for about 15 minutes or until pork is tender. Add salt and vinegar. Remove from heat.

7. Dish out and garnish as desired. Serve hot.

NOTE

· Do not be tempted to adjust the taste of the curry by adding more vinegar while the curry is still hot. When it is allowed to sit for a few minutes, the taste of the vinegar will kick in.

PORKU TAMBREYNO

Serves 6-8

Most sambals are prepared using a base of chillies, onions and the all-essential dried prawn (shrimp) paste (*belacan*), but *porku tambreyno* is a special sambal dish that is prepared without the use of the pungent dried paste. You will be surprised at the taste of this dish, as the slices of pork absorb the flavour of the sambal very well.

Pork knuckle 1 kg (2 lb 3 oz), thinly sliced

Ground white pepper $1/2$ Tbsp

Light soy sauce 1 Tbsp

Cooking oil 6 Tbsp

Onions 2, peeled and sliced into rings

Tamarind pulp 1 Tbsp, mixed with 2 Tbsp water and strained

Limes 3, juice extracted

Ground Paste

Dried chillies 100 g ($3^1/2$ oz), cut into short lengths, soaked for 10 minutes, seeds removed

Candlenuts 4

Coarse salt 1 Tbsp

1. Season pork with pepper and soy sauce and leave to marinate for 20 minutes.

2. Pound or grind together ingredients for ground paste coarsely.

3. Heat oil in a pot and fry ground paste until fragrant.

4. Add marinated pork and onion rings, then lower heat and cover pot with a lid. Leave to cook for 5 minutes.

5. Remove lid and mix ingredients in pot thoroughly. Stir in tamarind liquid and lime juice. Remove from heat.

6. Dish out and garnish as desired. Serve hot.

NOTE

· Always slice pork against the grain so that it will remain tender even after cooking.

BABI ASSAM

Serves 6-8

This is a very mild curry with tantalising flavours. My dad used to prepare it with pork trotters so the curry would be very *lemak* (rich) when the pork fat is rendered and infused with the other ingredients in the curry. In this recipe, I use pork leg instead of trotters.

Cooking oil 4 Tbsp

Large onion 1, peeled and sliced

Lemon grass 1 stalk, ends trimmed, outer leaves removed and bruised

Pork leg 1 kg (2 lb 3 oz), cut into 3-cm (1^1/$_4$-in) cubes

Potatoes 3, peeled and quartered

Water 50 ml (1^2/$_3$ fl oz)

Salt ^{1}/$_4$ Tbsp

Tamarind pulp 2 Tbsp, mixed with 2 Tbsp water and strained

Ground Paste

Large onions 6, peeled and sliced

Lemon grass 2 stalks, ends trimmed, outer leaves removed and sliced

Turmeric 10-cm (4-in) knob, peeled

Dried prawn (shrimp) paste (*belacan*) 100 g (3^1/$_2$ oz)

Dried chillies 50 g (1^2/$_3$ oz), cut into short lengths, soaked for 10 minutes, seeds removed

1. Pound or grind together ingredients for ground paste until fine. Set aside.

2. Heat oil in a pot and fry onion and lemon grass until onion is soft.

3. Add ground paste and fry until oil rises.

4. Add pork and potatoes and fry for about 3 minutes.

5. Add water and salt to taste and boil until potatoes are soft and the curry thickens. Stir in tamarind liquid. Remove from heat.

6. Dish out and serve hot.

NOTE

· To prepare this dish using pork trotters, proceed as above, but let the ingredients simmer until the pork is tender. Cut the potatoes in halves instead of quarters so they do not become mushy while the pork cooks.

AMBILLA LABU

Serves 6–8

This Eurasian curry is prepared using *labu* or bottle gourd, a popular vegetable in Indian cuisine. When cooked, the bottle gourd is meltingly delicious, and in this dish, it absorbs all the flavours of the curry, making this dish truly memorable.

Cooking oil 4 Tbsp

Large onion 1, peeled and sliced

Pork ribs 1 kg (2 lb 3 oz), cut into 4-cm (1^1/$_2$-in) pieces

Water 300 ml (10 fl oz / 1^1/$_4$ cups)

Bottle gourd 1 kg (2 lb 3 oz), peeled, cut into 8-cm (3-in) lengths and quartered

Salt ^{1}/$_4$ Tbsp

Tamarind pulp 2 Tbsp, mixed with 2 Tbsp water and strained

Ground Paste

Shallots 15, peeled

Onions 3, large, peeled and sliced

Turmeric 10-cm (4-in) knob, peeled

Dried prawn (shrimp) paste (*belacan*) 50 g (1^2/$_3$ oz)

Lemon grass 1 stalk, ends trimmed, outer leaves removed and sliced

Dried chillies 100 g (3^1/$_2$ oz), cut into short lengths, soaked for 10 minutes, seeds removed

1. Pound or grind together ingredients for ground paste until fine. Set aside.

2. Heat oil in a pot and fry onion until soft.

3. Add ground paste and fry until oil rises.

4. Add pork ribs and fry for 10 minutes.

5. Add water, bottle gourd and salt. Lower heat and simmer until pork is tender and curry thickens. This will take about 15 minutes.

6. Stir in tamarind liquid. Remove from heat.

7. Dish out and garnish as desired. Serve hot.

NOTE

· This curry can be kept in an airtight container in the refrigerator for up to 1 week.

FENG CURRY

Serves 8–10

The history of this dish goes back some 500 years. It was said that the Portuguese ships would carry livestock such as pigs so the crew would have fresh meat to eat during the voyage. The best cuts of meat were reserved for the officers while the poorer cuts and offals were chopped up, cooked into a stew and given to the deck hands. Spices were later added to the stew and it became what we know today as *feng* curry.

Cooking oil 6 Tbsp
Onions 3, peeled and diced
Ginger 100 g (3^1/$_2$ oz), peeled and diced
Light soy sauce 2 Tbsp
Water 200 ml (7 fl oz)
Salt ^{1}/$_2$ Tbsp
White vinegar 2 Tbsp

Pork

Water 1 litre (32 fl oz / 4 cups), mixed with 1 Tbsp salt and 3 Tbsp cooking oil
Pork shoulder 300 g (11 oz)
Pork belly 300 g (11 oz)
Pig's heart 200 g (7 oz)
Pig's liver 200 g (7 oz)
Pig's kidney 200 g (7 oz)

Spices

Cumin seeds 3 Tbsp
Fennel seeds 1 Tbsp
Coriander seeds 5 Tbsp
Black peppercorns 1 Tbsp
Aniseed 1 Tbsp
Cinnamon 1 stick, about 5-cm (2-in)
Cloves 4
Star anise 1

1. Using a spice mill, grind spices into a fine powder. Set aside.

2. Prepare pork. Boil water in a pot and blanch meats separately for 5 minutes each, ending with pig's kidney. Remove and drain. Cut meats into 0.5-cm (^{1}/$_4$-in) cubes. Set aside.

3. Heat oil in a pot and fry onions and ginger until oil rises and mixture is fragrant.

4. Add diced meats, soy sauce and water. Mix thoroughly and leave to boil until gravy thickens. Add salt and vinegar. Remove from heat.

5. Dish out and garnish as desired. Serve hot with warm French loaf or rice.

AMBILLA KACANG

Serves 6-8

At Quentin's, we named this beef and long bean curry Don's Ambilla Kacang after Don Nonis, a regular patron of the restaurant who frequently requested for this curry whenever he came to dine. This curry was not originally in the menu but because Don kept requesting for it, we finally added it to the menu.

Cooking oil 4 Tbsp

Large onion 1, peeled and sliced

Beef 1 kg (2 lb 3 oz), cut into 3-cm (1¹/₄-in) cubes

Water 300 ml (10 fl oz / 1¹/₄ cups)

Salt ¹/₄ Tbsp

Long beans 300 g (11 oz), cut into 5-cm (2-in) pieces

Tamarind pulp 2 Tbsp, mixed with 2 Tbsp water and strained

Ground Paste

Shallots 15, peeled

Large onions 3, peeled and sliced

Turmeric 10-cm (4-in) knob, peeled and sliced

Dried prawn (shrimp) paste (*belacan*) 50 g (1²/₃ oz)

Candlenuts 5

Lemon grass 1 stalk

Dried chillies 100 g (3¹/₂ oz), cut into short lengths, soaked for 10 minutes, seeds removed

1. Pound or grind together ingredients for ground paste until fine.

2. Heat oil in a pot over medium heat and fry onion until soft. Add ground paste and fry until oil rises.

3. Add beef and fry for about 5 minutes, then add water. Simmer until beef is tender and curry thickens. This will take about 20 minutes over medium heat.

4. Add long beans and simmer for 2 minutes. Stir in tamarind liquid. Remove from heat.

5. Dish out and garnish as desired. Serve hot.

NOTE

· To save on cooking time, a pressure cooker can be used to soften the beef if you have one. Follow the instructions on your pressure cooker.

BEEF STEAK

Serves 6-8

Although this recipe is called beef steak, the dish is not a steak. It is actually slices of beef fried with onions and dark sauce. I remember enjoying this dish whenever my dad cooked it, especially on Sundays when the whole family would gather together for dinner.

Beef fillet 1 kg (2 lb 3 oz), cut into
  0.5-cm ($^1/_4$-in) thick sliced

Ground black pepper 2 Tbsp + 1 Tbsp

Dark soy sauce 5 Tbsp + 4 Tbsp

Cooking oil as needed

Potatoes 4, peeled and cut into wedges

Water 50 ml ($1^2/_3$ fl oz)

Large onions 3, peeled and cut into
  0.5-cm ($^1/_4$-in) rounds

1. Place beef in a bowl with 2 Tbsp pepper and 5 Tbsp dark soy sauce. Mix well and leave to marinate for 20 minutes.

2. Heat enough oil for deep-frying and deep-fry potato wedges until golden brown. Drain well and set aside.

3. Heat 4 Tbsp oil in a wok and add marinated beef, 1 Tbsp pepper and 4 Tbsp dark soy sauce. Stir-fry for about 2 minutes.

4. Add water and simmer for about 2 minutes, then add onions and fried potato wedges. Bring to the boil and cook for another 5 minutes or until beef is tender.

5. Dish out and garnish as desired. Serve hot.

NOTE

· When slicing the beef, slice it against the grain. This will reduce the cooking time and ensure that the beef is tender and not tough when cooked.

SEAFOOD

SINGGANG SERANI

Serves 6–8

This is a runny curry with full flavours. The wolf herring or *ikan parang* was traditionally used for this dish, but as the wolf herring has many bones, other types of fish with firm white flesh can be used instead. The Eurasians often use dill as garnishing for seafood dishes. Try it for a taste of something different.

Cooking oil 4 Tbsp

Onion 1, peeled and sliced

Lemon grass 1 stalk, ends trimmed, tough outer leaves removed and sliced

Sugar 2 Tbsp

Light soy sauce 1 Tbsp

Water 700 ml (23$^1/_3$ fl oz / 2$^4/_5$ cups)

Wolf herring (*ikan parang*) 1, about 1 kg (2 lb 3 oz), cut into 5-cm (2-in) pieces

Salt $^1/_2$ Tbsp

Tamarind pulp 2 Tbsp, mixed with 2 Tbsp water and strained

Chilli Paste

Large onions 4, peeled and sliced

Dried chillies 20, cut into short lengths, soaked for 10 minutes, seeds removed

Dried prawn (shrimp) paste (*belacan*) 50 g (1$^2/_3$ oz)

Turmeric 4-cm (1$^1/_2$-in) knob, peeled and chopped

Lemon grass 3 stalks, ends trimmed, tough outer leaves removed and sliced

1. Pound or grind together ingredients for chilli paste until fine.

2. Heat oil in a pot and fry onion and lemon grass lightly. Add chilli paste and fry until fragrant. Add sugar and soy sauce and continue frying for 1 minute. Add water and bring to boil.

3. Add fish, lower heat and cover pot with a lid. Cook for 7 minutes, then add salt and tamarind liquid and return to the boil.

4. Dish out and garnish as desired. Serve hot.

NOTE

- When using wolf herring, it is always advisable to align the bones of the fish before cooking so the bones can be removed easily before eating. You do this by holding the head and tail of the fish firmly and stretching the fish.

PRAWN CHILLI GARAM

Serves 6–8

My memories of this dish go back to the 1970s when I was just a few years old. The beach was very close to our home and whenever the fishermen came back from their fishing trips, my dad would go over their catch to purchase fresh seafood. If there were prawns (shrimps), he would buy them and make this dish. It is a simple dish that brings out the natural sweetness and flavour of the prawns.

Cooking oil 6 Tbsp

Large prawns (shrimps) 1 kg (2 lb 3 oz), about 20–25 prawns, trimmed and deveined, leaving shells on

Chilli Paste

Dried chillies 100 g (3 1/2 oz), cut into short lengths, soaked for 10 minutes, seeds removed

Candlenuts 4

Coarse salt 1 Tbsp

Ground white pepper 1/2 Tbsp

Light soy sauce 1 Tbsp

1. Pound or grind together ingredients for chilli paste until fine.

2. Marinate prawns with 2 Tbsp chilli paste and set aside for 10 minutes.

3. Heat oil in a wok and fry remaining chilli paste for 1 minute.

4. Add marinated prawns and lower heat. Cover wok with a lid and cook for 5 minutes. Stir-fry to check that prawns have changed colour and are evenly cooked.

5. Dish out and garnish as desired. Serve hot.

NOTE

- To keep prawns fresh in the freezer, sprinkle them with 1 Tbsp sugar and 1 Tbsp salt and wrap with newspaper before freezing. The prawns will keep for up to 2 weeks.

PINEAPPLE PRAWN CURRY

Serves 6-8

There are many variations to this dish and the Malays and Peranakans also have their own way of preparing this dish. My personal favourite way of enjoying this dish is with a side dish of spicy chilli paste as shown below.

Ripe pineapple 1, medium

Cooking oil 4 Tbsp

Sugar 2 Tbsp

Light soy sauce 1 Tbsp

Water 500 ml (16 fl oz / 2 cups)

Large prawns (shrimps) 1 kg (2 lb 3 oz), about 20–25 prawns, trimmed and deveined, leaving heads and shells on

Salt 1/2 Tbsp

Tamarind pulp 1 Tbsp, mixed with 100 ml (3 1/2 fl oz) water and strained

Chilli Paste

Onions 3, peeled and sliced

Dried chillies 20, cut into short lengths, soaked for 10 minutes, seeds removed

Dried prawn (shrimp) paste (*belacan*) 50 g (1 2/3 oz)

Turmeric 5-cm (2-in) knob, peeled

Lemon grass 1 stalk, ends trimmed, hard outer leaves removed and sliced

Patah Chilli

Limes 2, juice extracted

Dark soy sauce 6 Tbsp

Red chillies 2

1. Cut stem off pineapple, then trim off skin and eyes. Cut pineapple in half, then slice into 1-cm (1/2-in) thick semi-circles. Set aside.

2. Pound or grind together ingredients for chilli paste until fine.

3. Prepare *patah* chilli. Mix lime juice and soy sauce in a small bowl, then break chillies into bowl. Set aside.

4. Heat oil in a pot and stir-fry chilli paste for about 1 minute.

5. Add sugar, soy sauce and pineapple pieces and stir-fry for another minute. Add water and bring to boil.

6. Add prawns, lower heat and cover pot with a lid. Leave for 5 minutes, then add salt and tamarind liquid and return to the boil.

7. Dish out and garnish as desired. Serve with *patah* chilli on the side.

PERMENTA FRIED PRAWNS

Serves 6–8

Also known as fried pepper prawns, this simple dish goes well with a plate of freshly cooked plain rice. The key to a perfect dish is to lightly cook the prawns so that they absorb the flavours of the other ingredients and still retain their natural juiciness and sweetness. Be careful not to overcook the prawns or they will be tough.

Large prawns (shrimps) 1 kg (2 lb 3 oz),
   about 20–25 prawns, peeled and deveined

Light soy sauce 3 Tbsp + 2 Tbsp

Ground white pepper 2 Tbsp

Lettuce 1 medium head, thinly sliced

Butter 3 Tbsp

Black peppercorns 50 g ($1^2/_3$ oz), crushed

Garlic 5 cloves, peeled and chopped

Water 100 ml ($3^1/_2$ fl oz)

Cornflour (cornstarch) $^1/_2$ Tbsp, mixed with
   2 Tbsp water

1. Place prawns in a bowl and marinate with 3 Tbsp soy sauce and ground white pepper. Set aside.

2. Arrange lettuce on a serving plate.

3. Heat butter in a wok and fry crushed peppercorns and garlic until garlic starts to brown.

4. Add marinated prawns, water and 2 Tbsp soy sauce. Lower heat and simmer for 5 minutes.

5. Add cornflour mixture and mix quickly, then dish out onto prepared serving plate. Serve hot.

NOTE

- This recipe requires slightly more butter to cook the prawns, but do not worry about the dish being too greasy as the layer of lettuce will absorb any excess melted butter from the prawns.

SOTONG BLACK

Serves 6-8

Sotong is the Malay work for squid. The name of this dish is derived from its colour, which is due to the ink of the squid. The Portuguese also have a similar dish in their repertoire, and this dish probably originated from there. The squid ink sauce will turn your teeth black, but the taste is worth it all!

Squid 1 kg (2 lb 3 oz)

Cooking oil 5 Tbsp

Onions 3, peeled and sliced

Garlic 10 cloves, peeled and sliced

Red chillies 5, sliced

Dark soy sauce 1 Tbsp

Water 3 Tbsp

Salt $^1/_2$ tsp

1. To clean squid, pull tail and tentacles apart. The head and innards will follow. Locate the silver coloured ink sac among the innards and be careful not to puncture it. Cut away eyes and innards from the area just behind the eyes and discard. Squeeze out beak from base of tentacles and discard. Remove quill from body of squid and discard. Wash squid tube and tentacles. Cut squid tube into rings. Set aside.

2. Heat oil in wok and fry onions, garlic and chillies until onions are soft.

3. Add squid, soy sauce, water and salt. Lower heat and cover wok with a lid. Simmer for 10 minutes or until gravy is thick and black.

4. Dish out and garnish as desired. Serve hot.

NOTE

· Depending on your taste preference, you may adjust the heat of this dish by adding more or less chillies as desired.

SOI LEMANG

Serves 4

This typical homestyle dish is best prepared with *ikan cincaru*, also known as hardtail fish. Cooked in a mouthwatering spicy and sour sauce, this dish goes well with a plate of freshly cooked white rice and a dish of sambal *belacan* (page 30) on the side. The skin of the hardtail fish is very tough and is usually not eaten. Peel it off and enjoy the firm and succulent flesh beneath.

Hardtail fish 4, each about 150 g (5^1/$_3$ oz)
  cleaned and gutted

Cooking oil 250 ml (8 fl oz / 1 cup)

Red chillies 2, sliced

Onions 4, peeled and cut into rings

Water 100 ml (3^1/$_2$ fl oz)

Light soy sauce 1 Tbsp

Dark soy sauce 2 Tbsp

Limes 6, juice extracted

Chilli Paste

Dried chillies 100 g (3^1/$_2$ oz), cut into
  short lengths, soaked for 10 minutes,
  seeds removed

Candlenuts 3

Salt ^{1}/$_2$ tsp

1. Pound or grind together ingredients for chilli paste until fine.

2. Using a small sharp knife, make a slit down the right and left side of the spine of each fish. Spoon 1 Tbsp chilli paste into the slits on each fish and place any remaining paste into the stomach of fish. Set aside for 10 minutes.

3. Heat 200 ml (7 fl oz) oil in a pan and pan-fry fish on one side until lightly brown and crisp. Repeat to cook the other side. Dish out and set aside.

4. Heat remaining oil in the pan and fry remaining chilli paste until oil rises.
   Add chillies, onions, water and soy sauces and let boil.

5. Return fried fish to pan. Drizzle over lime juice. Dish out and serve hot.

NOTE

· Depending on your taste preference, you may want to adjust the amount of lime juice added.
  Do this by adding a little lime juice at a time and tasting until you achieve the flavour desired.

CURRY MOOLIE

Serves 6-8

Curry *moolie* has its origins in India. It is a thick coconut based curry that can be enjoyed with bread or rice. The unique feature of this dish is the way the aubergines are prepared. The skin is completely peeled away, allowing the aubergines to become meltingly tender and to absorb the full flavour of the curry, making every mouthful a pleasure!

Round green aubergines
  (eggplants/brinjals) 2
Cooking oil 4 Tbsp
Onion $1/2$ peeled and sliced
Mackerel steaks 6, each about 120 g
  ($4^1/_3$ oz), cleaned
Water 300 ml (10 fl oz / $1^1/_4$ cups)
Coconut milk 100 ml ($3^1/_2$ fl oz)
Salt $1/_4$ Tbsp

Chilli Paste

Shallots 15, peeled
Large onions $2^1/_2$, peeled and sliced
Turmeric 8-cm (3-in) knob, peeled
  and chopped
Dried prawn (shrimp) paste (*belacan*)
  50 g ($1^2/_3$ oz)
Lemon grass 2 stalks, ends trimmed,
  tough outer leaves removed and sliced
Dried chillies 100 g ($3^1/_2$ oz), cut into
  short lengths, soaked for 10 minutes,
  seeds removed

1. Pound or grind together ingredients for chilli paste until fine. Set aside.

2. Wash aubergines and leave stems intact. Peel off skin using a vegetable peeler, then cut aubergines lengthwise into quarters without cutting through so the quarters are still held together by the stem.

3. Heat oil in a pot and fry onion until soft. Add chilli paste and fry until oil rises.

4. Add aubergines, fish and water. Lower heat and simmer until aubergines start to become tender, then add coconut milk and salt. Cook until curry is thickened.

5. Dish out and serve hot.

NOTE

· This dish can also be prepared with prawns instead of fish.

IKAN CHUAN CHUAN

Serves 4

This dish of fried pomfret in a sweet sour and spicy sauce was originally a Peranakan dish. It was adopted by the Eurasians and became a dish that was popularly prepared in Eurasian homes. While pomfret is the traditional fish used in this dish, you may also use other firm white flesh fish. My dad also uses red snapper (*ikan merah*).

Pomfrets 2, each about 300 g (11 oz), cleaned and gutted

Cooking oil 300 ml (10 fl oz / 1¼ cups)

Ginger 6-cm (2⅓-in) knob, peeled and cut into long, thin strips

Red chillies 2, sliced

Garlic 3 cloves, peeled and sliced

Onion 1, peeled and sliced

Water 3 Tbsp

Light soy sauce 1 Tbsp

Dark soy sauce 2 Tbsp

Sugar 1 Tbsp

Tamarind pulp 2 Tbsp, mixed with 3 Tbsp water and strained

Paste A

Dried chillies 15, cut and soaked for 10 minutes, seeds removed

Candlenuts 1

Salt ¼ tsp

Paste B

Garlic 6 cloves, peeled

Preserved soy bean paste (*taucheo*) 6 Tbsp

1. Pound or grind together ingredients for paste A until fine. Set aside.

2. Repeat to pound or grind together ingredients for paste B. Set aside.

3. Using a small sharp knife, make a slit down the right and left side of the spine of each fish. Spoon 1 Tbsp of paste A into the slits on each fish and place any remaining paste into the stomach of fish. Set aside for 10 minutes.

4. Heat 250 ml (8 fl oz / 1 cup) oil in a pan and pan-fry fish on one side until lightly brown and crisp. Repeat to cook the other side. Dish out to a serving plate.

5. Heat remaining oil in the pan and fry paste B until fragrant. Add ginger, chillies, garlic and onion and fry until onion is soft. Add water, soy sauces and sugar and let boil. Add tamarind liquid and return to boil.

6. Ladle sauce over fried fish. Garnish as desired and serve hot.

NOTE

- When frying fish, always leave one side to cook completely before turning the fish over to cook the other side. This will keep the fish from breaking up.

CAKES & DESSERTS

SAGO GULA MELAKA

Serves 6-8

This dessert is put together using just four simple ingredients—sago pearls, palm sugar, coconut milk and pandan leaves. It is a popular dessert in Singapore and Malaysia and some other countries in South East Asia as well. It can be quickly and easily put together for a light ending to a meal and can also be served as a snack at any time of the day. Adjust the sweetness of the dessert by adding palm sugar syrup to taste. Serve over ice cubes if desired.

Water as needed
Small sago pearls 300 g (11 oz)
Water 150 ml (5 fl oz)
Pandan leaves 3, cleaned and knotted
Palm sugar (*gula melaka*) 300 g (11 oz)
Grated coconut 600 g (1 lb 5¹/₃ oz)
Salt a pinch

1. Boil 1 litre (32 fl oz / 4 cups) water in a medium pot. Add sago, stirring constantly to ensure that beads do not stick together. When sago becomes translucent, add cool water to the pot and remove from heat. Pour sago into a large strainer and wash under running water to remove as much starch as possible. Refrigerate to chill.

2. Boil 150 ml (5 fl oz) water in a small pot. Add pandan leaves and palm sugar and continue boiling until sugar is dissolved. Remove from heat and strain. Refrigerate to chill.

3. Mix grated coconut with 100 ml (3¹/₂ fl oz) warm water. Place into a muslin cloth and squeeze out as much coconut milk as you can. Add a pinch of salt to coconut milk and stir thoroughly. Refrigerate to chill.

4. To serve, spoon a portion of sago into a bowl or glass. Drizzle with palm sugar and coconut milk.

WATERMELON, HONEYDEW AND SAGO IN COCONUT MILK

Serves 8-10

This light and refreshing dessert is a favourite with many. In my growing up years, this dessert was popularly served at parties, one reason being that it could be easily put together. Some recipes omit the watermelon, but it adds colour to an otherwise pale-looking dish.

Small sago pearls 100 g (3^1/$_2$ oz)

Grated coconut 1 kg (2 lb 3 oz)

Salt a pinch

Pandan leaves 3, cleaned and knotted

Sugar 100 g (3^1/$_2$ oz)

Evaporated milk 100 ml (3^1/$_2$ fl oz)

Seedless red watermelon ^{1}/$_2$, medium, flesh cut into 1-cm (^{1}/$_2$-in) cubes

Honeydew 1, medium, flesh cut into 1-cm (^{1}/$_2$-in) cubes

Ice cubes as needed

1. Boil 1 litre (32 fl oz / 4 cups) water in a medium pot. Add sago, stirring constantly to ensure that beads do not stick together. When sago becomes translucent, add cool water to the pot and remove from heat. Pour sago into a large strainer and wash under running water to remove as much starch as possible. Refrigerate to chill.

2. Mix grated coconut with 100 ml (3^1/$_2$ fl oz) warm water. Place into a muslin cloth and squeeze out as much coconut milk as you can. Add a pinch of salt to coconut milk and stir thoroughly.

3. Heat coconut milk in a pot over low heat. Add pandan leaves and sugar and stir constantly until sugar is dissolved. Add evaporated milk and leave to cool.

4. Place cut fruit and sago in a large bowl and pour over coconut milk mixture. Stir to mix. Refrigerate until needed.

5. Serve with ice cubes in serving bowls or glasses.

PULUT HITAM

Serves 8–10

Many know this dessert to be Peranakan, but this black glutinous rice pudding is also a popular dessert among the Eurasians. While the popular versions of this dessert is served simply sweetened with palm sugar and flavoured with coconut milk, this Eurasian recipe features cubed sweet potatoes for added taste and texture.

Black glutinous rice 500 g (1 lb 1^1/$_2$ oz), washed and soaked for at least 30 minutes

Pandan leaves 6, cleaned and knotted

Water 1 litre (32 fl oz / 4 cups)

Rock sugar 100 g (3^1/$_2$ oz)

Sweet potatoes 2, peeled and cut into 1-cm (^{1}/$_2$-in) cubes

Grated coconut 1 kg (2 lb 3 oz)

Salt a pinch

1. Place glutinous rice, pandan leaves and 500 ml (16 fl oz / 2 cups) water in a pot and bring to boil. As the rice cooks, add the remaining water gradually. This will ensure that the grains retain a firm texture. The glutinous rice should start to soften after about 20 minutes.

2. Add rock sugar and sweet potatoes and continue boiling until sweet potatoes are soft. Add a little more water if mixture is too thick.

3. As sweet potatoes are cooking, mix grated coconut with 100 ml (3^1/$_2$ fl oz) warm water. Place into a muslin cloth and squeeze out as much coconut milk as you can.

4. Add coconut milk and salt to pot. Stir to mix and serve immediately.

NOTE

· As coconut milk spoils easily, stir it into the cooked rice only when you are ready to serve.

BUBUR TERIGU

Serves 8–10

This tasty sweet porridge is made using white wheat or *terigu*. The Indonesian word, *terigu*, comes from *trigo*, the Portuguese word for wheat. The grains of white wheat resemble barley when uncooked and have an interesting bite when cooked. To shorten the cooking time, soak the grains for several hours before boiling.

Grated coconut 1 kg (2 lb 3 oz)

Salt a pinch

Water 500 ml (16 fl oz / 2 cups)

White wheat (*terigu*) 500 g (1 lb 1^1/$_2$ oz),
   washed and soaked for at least 6 hours

Pandan leaves 6, cleaned and knotted

Rock sugar 100 g (3^1/$_2$ oz)

1. Mix grated coconut with 100 ml (3^1/$_2$ fl oz) warm water. Place into a muslin cloth and squeeze out as much coconut milk as you can. Add a pinch of salt to coconut milk and stir thoroughly. Set aside.

2. Boil water in a pot and add white wheat and pandan leaves. Return to the boil, stirring occasionally, until white wheat starts to break up and mixture thickens.

3. Add rock sugar and stir until dissolved. Add a little more water if mixture becomes too thick.

4. Remove from heat. Stir in coconut milk and serve immediately.

NOTE

· Taste and adjust the sweetness of the dessert by adding some granulated sugar if desired. As coconut milk tends to spoil easily, stir it into the dessert just before serving.

KUEH KO SWEE

Makes one 20-cm (8-in) square cake

This is another dessert that is popularly known to be Peranakan, but the Eurasians have a version of it too. Peranakan *kueh ko swee* is prepared using tapioca flour and is flavoured using the juice of pandan leaves. The Eurasian recipe uses sago flour and the pandan leaves are boiled with the palm sugar. The Peranakans also traditionally steam the *kueh* in Chinese teacups while the Eurasians steam it as a whole cake in a baking tray.

Plain (all-purpose) flour 175 g ($6^1/_4$ oz)
Sago flour 100 g ($3^1/_2$ oz)
Grated skinned coconut 600 g (1 lb $5^1/_3$ oz)
Salt a pinch
Water 150 ml (5 fl oz)
Pandan leaves 3, cleaned and knotted
Palm sugar (*gula melaka*) 350 g ($12^1/_2$ oz)
Sugar 175 g ($6^1/_4$ oz)
Alkaline water 2 Tbsp

1. Sift together plain flour and sago flour and set aside.
2. Steam grated coconut for 5 minutes. When cool, mix in salt. Set aside to cool.
3. Boil 150 ml (5 fl oz) water in a small pot. Add pandan leaves, palm sugar and sugar and continue boiling until both types of sugar are dissolved. Remove from heat and strain.
4. Add alkaline water and mix well. Add sifted flour mixture and stir until there are no lumps.
5. Strain mixture into 20 x 20 x 5-cm (8 x 8 x 2-in) baking tin. Place into a steamer and steam for 40 minutes or until *kueh* is no longer opaque in colour.
6. To serve, cut *kueh* into rectangles or squares. Coat with steamed grated coconut just before serving.

NOTE

- If sago flour is not available, substitute with tapioca flour.

PUTUGAL

Makes one 25-cm (10-in) square cake

This recipe for steamed grated tapioca with grated coconut and banana was given to me by Mrs Lena Fox. According to her, this dessert was a favourite among the Eurasians. It was typically served during funeral wakes, so those who came to pay their respect would have something to eat, and as a result, stay on to keep the family company for longer.

Grated skinned coconut 400 g (14^1/$_3$ oz)

Sugar 1 Tbsp + 100 g (3^1/$_2$ oz)

Water 250 ml (8 fl oz / 1 cup)

Grated tapioca 300 g (11 oz)

Blue food colouring ^{1}/$_2$ tsp

Green food colouring ^{1}/$_2$ tsp

Banana leaf 1

Ripe bananas (*pisang rajah*) 5

1. Steam half the grated coconut. Leave to cool, then add 1 Tbsp sugar and mix well. Keep refrigerated until needed.

2. Mix remaining grated coconut with 125 ml (4 fl oz / ^{1}/$_2$ cup) water. Place into a muslin cloth and squeeze out about 125 ml (4 fl oz / ^{1}/$_2$ cup) coconut milk.

3. Add remaining water to grated tapioca and drain liquid into a bowl. Set aside grated tapioca and let drained liquid settle. Drain water, leaving starch at the bottom of bowl.

4. Mix grated tapioca, coconut milk, sugar and starch thoroughly. Divide into 2 portions. Divide the first portion in half and mix one part with blue food colouring and the other half with green food colouring. Leave other portion colourless.

5. Line a 25-cm (10-in) square baking tin with the banana leaf. Scoop 4 heaped tablespoons of blue coloured mixture into 4 corners of tray, then repeat to do the same with the green coloured mixture followed by the colourless mixture. Allow the colourless mixture to fill the gaps between the coloured mixtures.

6. Peel and slice bananas diagonally into 1-cm (^{1}/$_2$-in) thick slices. Insert banana slices randomly into mixture, then use the back of a spoon to smoothen out the surface.

7. Place into a steamer and steam for 20 minutes. Remove from heat and let cool.

8. Cut cake into diamond shapes. Coat with steamed grated coconut before serving.

NOTE

· *Pisang rajah* is traditionally used in this cake, but other varieties of banana such as *pisang kapok* and *pisang tanduk,* which are usually used for frying, can also be used.

· Grated tapioca is available from supermarkets.

KUEH BINGKA

Makes one 25-cm (10-in) square cake

This baked grated tapioca and coconut cake is popular throughout South East Asia and there are many variations to the recipe. Despite the many different recipes for this cake, a good *kueh bingka* is one where you can still taste the crunchiness of the grated coconut.

Plain (all-purpose) flour 150 g (5^1/$_3$ oz)

Baking powder 1 Tbsp

Eggs 4

Castor sugar 450 g (1 lb)

Grated tapioca 1 kg (2 lb 3 oz)

Grated skinned coconut 400 g (14^1/$_3$ oz)

Yellow food colouring ^{1}/$_2$ Tbsp

Vanilla extract ^{1}/$_2$ Tbsp

Coconut milk 250 ml (8 fl oz / 1 cup)

Cooking oil 3 Tbsp + more for greasing tray

Salt a pinch

1. Sift together flour and baking powder. Set aside.

2. Preheat oven to 170°C (330°F). Grease a 25-cm (10-in) square baking tin.

3. Beat eggs and sugar in mixing bowl until creamy.

4. Add grated tapioca and grated coconut and mix well.

5. Add sifted flour, food colouring, vanilla extract, coconut milk and oil. Mix everything together well.

6. Pour mixture into prepared tin and spread evenly. Bake for 1 hour or until set and top of cake is lightly browned.

7. Leave to cool completely before cutting to serve. This cake will keep in an airtight container in the refrigerator for up to 3 days.

TAPIOCA AND COCONUT CAKE

Makes one 20-cm (8-in) square cake

This seems to be a variation of *kueh bingka* (page 138), made without eggs or flour. It is also steamed instead of baked and is hence suitable for those who do not have an oven at home. I enjoy it for its lighter texture and it can be served as dessert even after a substantial meal.

Grated skinned coconut 400 g (14^1/$_3$ oz)

Salt ^{1}/$_4$ Tbsp

Water 250 ml (8 fl oz / 1 cup)

Palm sugar (*gula melaka*) 100 g (3^1/$_2$ oz)

Tapioca 1 kg (2 lb 3 oz)

Cooking oil 1 Tbsp

1. Steam half the grated coconut. Leave to cool, then add salt and mix well. Keep refrigerated until needed.

2. Boil water with palm sugar, stirring until sugar is dissolved. Strain syrup.

3. Peel tapioca and cut into 3-cm (1^1/$_4$-in) pieces. Wash and drain, then steam for 20 minutes. Remove from heat and mash immediately with remaining uncooked grated coconut.

4. Grease a 20-cm (8-in) square baking tin with oil. Spread mixture out in tin and steam for 20 minutes. Remove from heat and leave to cool.

5. Cut cake into diamond shapes. Coat with steamed grated coconut just before serving.

PINEAPPLE TARTS

Makes about 100 small tarts

In Singapore, pineapple tarts are the quintessential festive treat. The Chinese and Peranakans prepare them for the Chinese new year festivities, the Malays for Hari Raya and the Eurasians for Christmas. Every year, my extended family would gather to make pineapple tarts just before Christmas. For Eurasians, the ideal pastry is firm but melts in the mouth. During these baking sessions, my sister takes charge of making the pastry, my dad the *kincha* (jam) and the rest of us would cut the dough and assemble the tarts.

Ripe pineapples 5, medium

Sugar 600 g (1 lb 5^1/$_3$ oz)

Cinnamon stick 1, about 5-cm (2-in)

Star anise 1

Cloves 10 g (^{1}/$_3$ oz)

Egg 1, beaten, for glazing tarts

Dough

Plain (all-purpose) flour 1 kg (2 lb 3 oz)

Chilled butter 500 g (1 lb 1^1/$_2$ oz), cut into cubes

Egg yolks from 4 eggs

Egg whites from 3 eggs

Iced water 2 tsp, mixed with 1 tsp salt

1. Cut stem off pineapples, then trim off skin and eyes. Cut pineapples into wedges and grate. Place in a colander and leave to drain.

2. Place grated pineapple, sugar, cinnamon stick, star anise and cloves in a pot and cook over low heat, stirring constantly for about 2 hours until jam is dry and golden brown. Set aside.

3. Prepare dough. Sift flour in a bowl. Add butter and rub flour into butter with finger tips until crumbly.

4. Add egg yolks, egg whites and iced water. Mix well.

5. Roll dough out into a thin sheet on a floured work surface. Using a small tart cutter, cut dough into rounds, then pinch the edges using pastry clippers.

6. Preheat oven to 170°C (330°F). Grease 2–3 baking trays with butter.

7. Take a spoonful of jam and place on top of each round of dough. Brush with beaten egg and arrange on baking trays. Cut shapes from excess pastry and use to decorate tarts if desired.

8. Bake tarts for 30 minutes or until golden brown. Transfer to a wire rack to cool completely. Store in an airtight container for up to 1 month.

NOTE

· Leave the grated pineapple to drain in the colander for as long as you can. This will help to shorten the cooking time.

BREAD PUDDING

Makes one 20-cm (8-in) square cake

Whenever my mum makes sandwiches for a party, she will also make bread pudding from the bread crusts, which she trims from the sandwiches. Bread pudding is good on its own, but can also be served with custard. To add some crunch to the bread pudding, roasted sliced almonds can be sprinkled over as garnish.

Sliced white bread 200 g (7 oz)
Raisins 2 Tbsp
Sugar 2 Tbsp
Grated nutmeg $1/2$ tsp
Milk 300 ml (10 fl oz / $1^1/_4$ cups)
Egg 1
Vanilla extract $1/2$ Tbsp
Brandy 1 Tbsp

1. Grease a 20-cm (8-in) square baking tin with butter.
2. Line pan with half the number of slices of bread. The bread can be sliced to fill the tray.
3. Sprinkle half the raisins, half the sugar and half the grated nutmeg over, then cover with remaining slices of bread, followed by remaining raisins, sugar and nutmeg.
4. Pour milk into a bowl and add egg, vanilla extract and brandy. Mix thoroughly. Pour mixture over bread and leave it to soak for 45 minutes.
5. Bake pudding in an oven preheated to 160°C (325°F) for 30 minutes.
6. Unmould pudding onto a large serving plate. Slice and serve warm.

KUEH KO CHEE

Makes 15 parcels

Kueh ko chee or Passover cake was traditionally made using ground unpolished glutinous rice and sweet potatoes, with a filling of grated coconut. To the Eurasians, the dark colour of the dough from the unpolished rice symbolises death and the sweet filling within, resurrection. This cake was usually served at funerals. As it became difficult to find ground unpolished glutinous rice, the recipe was adapted to use glutinous rice flour, and half the dough was coloured blue to maintain the pattern of colours in the original cake.

Banana leaves 4–5
Sweet potatoes 200 g (7 oz)
Glutinous rice flour 350 g (12^1/$_2$ oz)
Cooking oil 2 Tbsp
Sugar 1 Tbsp
Salt ^{1}/$_4$ tsp
Blue food colouring ^{1}/$_2$ tsp

Filling
Grated skinned coconut 300 g (11 oz)
Palm sugar (*gula melaka*) 150 g (5^1/$_3$ oz), grated
Salt ^{1}/$_4$ tsp
Cooking oil 1 Tbsp

Coconut Milk
Grated coconut 600 g (1 lb 5^1/$_3$ oz)
Warm water 100 ml (3^1/$_2$ fl oz)

1. Using a 20-cm (8-in) round cake tin as a guide, cut 15 rounds from banana leaves. Scald over an open flame or steam to soften leaves and make them pliable. Set aside.

2. Prepare filling. Cook grated coconut, palm sugar, salt and cooking oil in a pot over low heat until sugar is dissolved and mixture is dry. Set aside to cool.

3. Boil a pot of water and cook sweet potatoes until tender. Peel and mash finely, then mix with 200 g (7 oz) glutinous rice flour until mixture is crumbly. Set aside.

4. Prepare coconut milk. Mix grated coconut with warm water. Place into a muslin cloth and squeeze to extract as much coconut milk as you can.

5. Place coconut milk, oil, sugar and salt in a pot and heat until sugar is dissolved. Add remaining glutinous rice flour and mix well. Remove from heat and add to sweet potato mixture. Knead together to form a soft dough. The dough should not be sticky.

6. Divide dough into 2 portions. Mix blue colouring into one portion and knead well, leaving the other potion plain.

7. Pat down each portion of dough into a flat rectangular sheet. Place blue coloured dough on top of the plain dough and roll up tightly like a Swiss roll. Cut rolled dough into 15 equal portions.

8. Using fingers, flatten a portion of dough, then place 1 Tbsp filling in the centre. Bring edges of dough up and pinch to enclose filling. Repeat until ingredients are used up.

9. Fold a banana leaf into a cone and place a ball of dough inside. Fold edge of leaf in to enclose dough. Repeat with remaining ingredients.

10. Place parcels in a steamer and steam for 15 minutes over high heat. Serve warm.

NOTE

- Traditionally, blue colouring was extracted from dried *bunga telang* (Clitoria ternatea). If you are able to obtain the dried flowers, soak 2–3 in 100 ml (3^1/$_2$ fl oz) water for at least 15 minutes and strain before use.

FESTIVE DISHES

BIRTHDAY MEE

Serves 6-8

This dish of birthday *mee* is also known as longevity noodles or *mee Serani* (Eurasian *mee*). As its various names suggest, this dish is typically served on birthdays as it is believed to represent longevity, hence the strands of noodles are traditionally not cut but kept long. The Eurasians always serve this dish with sambal *acar nanas* (page 36).

Prawns (shrimps) 300 g (11 oz)

Squid 300 g (11 oz)

Cooking oil 6 Tbsp

Pork belly 200 g (7 oz), cut into thin strips

Salt 1/4 Tbsp

Light soy sauce 1 Tbsp

Water 100 ml (3 1/2 fl oz)

Fresh yellow noodles 1 kg (2 lb 3 oz)

Chinese flowering cabbage (*chye sim*)
  200 g (7 oz)

Bean sprouts 300 g (11 oz)

Red chilli 1, sliced

Coriander leaves (cilantro) 5 sprigs

Cucumber 1/2, cut into long thin trips

Paste

Garlic 6 cloves, peeled and chopped

Preserved soy bean paste (*taucheo*)
  6 Tbsp

1. Peel prawns, leaving tails intact. Slit prawns along the back and remove the black intestine. Rinse well and pat dry.

2. To clean squid, firmly pull head and body tube apart. The head and innards should slip out of the body. Trim off innards by cutting below the eyes. Discard. Squeeze between the eyes to remove the beak (which is located at the base of the tentacles) and discard. Remove cartilage from inside body and discard. Rinse squid and cut into rings about 1-cm (1/2-in) thick.

3. Mash garlic and fermented soy bean paste together.

4. Heat oil in a wok and fry paste with pork belly, prawns and squid until oil rises. Add salt, soy sauce and water and bring to boil.

5. Add noodles, Chinese flowering cabbage and bean sprouts. Mix thoroughly and cook for 3 minutes. Remove from heat.

6. Garnish with sliced chilli, coriander and cucumber. Serve hot.

NOTE

· Slices of plain omelette are sometimes added as a garnish. To do this, beat 2-3 eggs together and cook into thin omelettes in a lightly oiled frying pan. Roll up the omelette and slice thinly.

CURRY DEBAL

Serves 6-8

Curry *debal* or curry devil is perhaps one of the most popular dishes in the Eurasian food repertoire. Every Eurasian family will have their own version of this dish and my family's recipe was passed down from my grandmother. *Debal* means leftovers in Creole-Portuguese as this curry was actually prepared with leftovers, but as not everyone understood what *debal* meant, reference was made to the heat of the dish and it became known as curry devil.

Chicken 1, about 1.5 kg (3 lb 4$^1/_2$ oz), cut into pieces

Light soy sauce 4 Tbsp

Ground white pepper 2 Tbsp

Cooking oil 5 Tbsp

Onion 1, peeled and halved; $^1/_2$ thinly sliced and $^1/_2$ quartered

Ginger 3-cm (1$^1/_4$-in) knob, peeled and cut into thin strips

Bacon bones 200 g (7 oz)

Mustard seeds 1 Tbsp, roughly pounded

Salt $^1/_2$ Tbsp

Crushed chicken stock cube $^1/_2$ Tbsp

Potatoes 2, peeled and quartered

Chicken cocktail sausages 10

Water 700 ml (23$^1/_2$ fl oz)

Cabbage $^1/_2$ head

Cucumber 1, peeled, cut into quarters lengthwise, soft centres removed and cut into 5-cm (2-in) lengths

White vinegar 5 Tbsp

Red bird's eye chillies 6–8

Ground Paste

Shallots 15, peeled

Large onions 5, peeled and sliced

Ginger 10-cm (4-in) knob, peeled and sliced

Red chillies 10

Dried chillies 50 g (1$^2/_3$ oz), cut into short lengths, soaked for 10 minutes, seeds removed

1. Season chicken with soy sauce and pepper and leave to marinate for 20 minutes.

2. Pound or grind together ingredients for ground paste until fine. Set aside.

3. Heat oil in a pot over medium heat and fry thinly sliced onion and ginger until light brown.

4. Add marinated chicken and bacon bones and continue frying until chicken changes colour.

5. Add ground paste, mustard seeds, salt and chicken stock and fry until oil rises.

6. Add potatoes, cocktail sausages and water. Boil until potatoes are soft and curry is thickened. This will take about 10 minutes on medium heat.

7. Add cabbage, cucumber and vinegar and mix well. Remove from heat.

8. Dish out and serve hot, garnished with whole bird's eye chillies.

NOTE

· This curry can be prepared days ahead without the vegetables and kept in an airtight container in the refrigerator. Add the vegetables only when reheating to serve.

BAKED BROCCOLI AND CAULIFLOWER

Serves 6–8

This vegetable dish is great for parties as you can prepare it in advance, and then just place it in the oven to cook just before the party. To make this dish a winner, ensure that the ingredients are well covered with cheese.

Broccoli 400 g (14$^1/_3$ oz), cut into florets

Cauliflower 400 g (14$^1/_3$ oz), cut into florets

Carrots 100 g (3$^1/_2$ oz), peeled and sliced

Canned button mushrooms 250 g (9 oz), drained and quartered

Black peppercorns 1 Tbsp, coarsely ground

Sea salt 1 Tbsp

Italian herbs or mixed herbs 1 Tbsp

Olive oil 4 Tbsp

Onions 2, peeled and quartered

Garlic 4 cloves, peeled and sliced

Cheddar or mozzarella cheese 12 slices

1. Preheat oven to 160°C (325°F).

2. Place broccoli, cauliflower, carrots and mushrooms in a 20-cm (8-in) casserole dish. Add ground peppercorns, sea salt, herbs, olive oil, onions and garlic. Mix thoroughly.

3. Cover vegetables with cheese, then cover casserole with aluminium foil. Place in the oven and bake for 30 minutes.

4. Remove aluminium foil and increase oven heat to 180°C (350°F). Leave vegetables to bake for another 10 minutes.

5. Remove from oven and serve hot.

POT ROAST BEEF

Serves 6–8

Pot roast beef is a chunk of beef knuckle, slowly roasted in a pot. The beef may take a long time to cook, but the result is worth the wait. Due to the long cooking process, this dish is typically reserved for special occasions such as Christmas and New Year.

Beef knuckle 2 kg (4 lb 6 oz)

Cooking oil 100 ml (3^1/$_2$ fl oz)

Onion 1, peeled and sliced

Beef stock cubes 2

Black peppercorns 3 Tbsp, coarsely ground

Water 1 litre (32 fl oz / 4 cups)

Baby carrots 300 g (11 oz)

Baby potatoes 300 g (11 oz)

Canned button mushrooms 325 g (11^2/$_3$ oz)

Ground Paste

Onions 800 g (1^3/$_4$ lb)

Dark soy sauce 6 Tbsp

Ground black pepper 5 Tbsp

Sugar 2 Tbsp

1. Pound or grind together ingredients for ground paste until fine.

2. Rub beef knuckle with 10 Tbsp ground paste and set aside for 1 hour.

3. Heat oil in a pot and sear marinated beef on all sides. Remove and set aside.

4. Reheat pot and fry onion until soft. Add remaining ground paste and fry until fragrant. Add beef stock cubes, ground peppercorns and water and bring to boil.

5. Add beef to pot and return to boil. Cover pot with a lid and simmer over low heat for 1^1/$_2$ hours, turning beef over every 20 minutes or so.

6. Add carrots, potatoes and mushrooms and continue boiling for another 20 minutes. Remove from heat and let cool slightly.

7. Remove beef and slice thinly. Arrange on serving plates and ladle gravy over beef. Serve carrots, potatoes and mushrooms on the side.

NOTE

· If desired, a can of cola may be added to the ground paste instead of sugar. The cola will not only add sweetness to the dish, but also help tenderise the beef as it cooks.

PRAWN BASTADOR

Serves 6-8

How did this dish get its name? *Bostador* literally means slap in Creole-Portuguese and this dish of prawns and green chillies used to be served as a sandwich filling. When the unsuspecting diner bit into a chilli, the heat was just like getting slapped in the face! This dish is now more often served as a side dish with rice. To serve it as a sandwich filling, peel the prawns and chop them into small cubes before cooking.

Cooking oil 2 Tbsp

Onion $1/2$, peeled and thinly sliced

Salt $1/4$ Tbsp

Chicken stock cube 1

Prawns (shrimps) 1 kg (2 lb 3 oz), about 20–25 prawns, peeled and deveined, leaving tails intact

Water 100 ml ($3^1/2$ fl oz)

Coconut milk 100 ml ($3^1/2$ fl oz)

Green chillies 5, stems removed and sliced

Chilli Paste

Shallots 15, peeled and sliced

Onions 2, peeled and sliced

Turmeric 5-cm (2-in), peeled

Dried prawn (shrimp) paste (*belacan*) 30 g (1 oz)

Candlenut 1

Dried chillies 20, cut into short lengths, soaked for 10 minutes, seeds removed

1. Pound or grind together ingredients for chilli paste until fine.

2. Heat oil in a pot and fry onion until soft. Add chilli paste, salt and chicken stock cube and fry until fragrant.

3. Add prawns and water stir-fry until prawns change colour and are cooked. Add coconut milk and bring to boil. Add green chillies and stir thoroughly.

4. Remove from heat and serve hot.

PANG SUSIE

Makes about 40 buns

Pang susie is a must-have for any Eurasian tea party. The filling is traditionally made with pork but can be substituted with chicken if desired. These buns are sometimes also made with sweet potato flour, but my preference is to use mashed sweet potatoes as it gives the buns more bite and texture.

Dough

Plain (all-purpose) flour 500 g (1 lb 1^1/$_2$ oz)

Instant yeast 1 sachet, 11 g (^{1}/$_3$ oz)

Sugar 100 g (3^1/$_2$ oz)

Butter 125 g (4^1/$_2$ oz)

Egg yolks from 2 eggs

Evaporated milk 50 ml (1^2/$_3$ fl oz)

Brandy 2 Tbsp

Sweet potatoes 400 g (14^1/$_3$ oz), boiled, peeled and mashed

Filling

Cooking oil 4 Tbsp

Onions 100 g (3^1/$_2$ oz), peeled and diced

Minced pork 600 g (1 lb 5^1/$_3$ oz)

Dark soy sauce 1 Tbsp

Light soy sauce 1 Tbsp

Sugar ^{1}/$_2$ Tbsp

Salt ^{1}/$_4$ Tbsp

Spices

Black peppercorns 1 Tbsp

Cinnamon 1 stick, about 1.5-cm (^{3}/$_4$-in)

Ground nutmeg ^{1}/$_2$ Tbsp

Cloves 5

Star anise 1

Egg Glaze

Egg yolk from 1 egg, beaten

1. Prepare dough. Sift flour and yeast into a mixing bowl and add sugar. Add butter and egg yolks and rub in with fingers until mixture is crumbly. Add evaporated milk, brandy and mashed sweet potato. Continue mixing until smooth and soft dough is formed.

2. Shape dough into a ball and place it in a mixing bowl. Cover bowl with a damp cloth and refrigerate for at least 1 hour for dough to rise.

3. Using a spice mill, grind spices into a fine powder. Set aside.

4. Prepare filling. Heat oil in a pot over medium heat and fry onions until soft. Add pork, soy sauces, sugar, salt and $^1/_4$ Tbsp ground spices. Fry for about 5 minutes, then set aside to cool.

5. Grease 2–3 baking trays and set aside. Preheat oven to 190°C (370°F).

6. Divide dough into 40 g ($1^1/_3$ oz) portions. Using your fingers, flatten a portion into an oval shape.

7. Spoon 1 Tbsp filling onto dough and enclose by bringing edges of dough together and pinching to secure. Repeat until ingredients are used up.

8. Place buns pinched side down on a greased baking tray, spacing them about 5-cm (2-in) apart.

9. Bake buns for about 15 minutes or until golden brown. As soon as you remove the tray from the oven, brush the buns with beaten egg yolk.

10. Leave buns to cool before serving.

SUGEE CAKE

Makes one 25-cm (10-in) square cake

Made from semolina and almonds, sugee cake was the cake of choice for celebrations among the Eurasians. It was covered with marzipan and decorated royal icing for occasions such as weddings, anniversaries and baptisms. For weddings, the cake would be made with three tiers, with the top tier reserved for the bride and groom to take home and enjoy.

Almonds 500 g (1 lb 1$\frac{1}{2}$ oz)

Semolina 500 g (1 lb 1$\frac{1}{2}$ oz)

Butter 500 g (1 lb 1$\frac{1}{2}$ oz), melted

Egg whites 375 g (13$\frac{1}{3}$ oz)

Castor sugar 500 g (1 lb 1$\frac{1}{2}$ oz)

Egg yolks 225 g (8 oz)

Baking powder 6 tsp

Vanilla extract 1 Tbsp

Brandy 4 Tbsp

1. Start preparations a day ahead. Soak almonds in hot water and peel off skin. Drain and spread out to dry on a tray. Place semolina in a container and mix thoroughly with melted butter.

2. The following day, preheat oven to 140°C (284°F). Line and grease a 25-cm (10-in) square baking tin.

3. Grind almonds coarsely.

4. Whisk egg whites until stiff peaks form.

5. In a separate bowl, whisk sugar and egg yolks at high speed for 5 minutes. Using a spatula, fold in semolina and half the whisked egg whites by hand. Fold in ground almonds and remaining whisked egg whites until incorporated. Fold in baking powder, vanilla extract and brandy and continue mixing until batter is uniform.

6. Pour batter into tray and bake for 75 minutes or until cake is done. Leave cake to cool before unmoulding.

NOTE

- To check that the cake is done, insert a skewer or very thin knife into the centre of the cake for a second or two and then remove. If the cake mixture is still wet and sticks to the blade, the cake needs a few more minutes in the oven. If the blade comes out clean, the cake is ready.

- Sugee cake can be stored for months in the freezer. To thaw, remove from the freezer and leave at room temperature for 8–10 hours before serving.

GLOSSARY OF
INGREDIENTS

ALKALINE WATER Known locally as lye water or *kan-sui,* this colourless alkaline solution contains potassium carbonate and sodium bicarbonate. It is used in making noodles and Asian snacks (*kuehs*) to give the final products a firmer texture and their characteristic yellow colour.

ASSAM GELUGOR SLICES, DRIED The *assam gelugor* fruit tree is native to Peninsular Malaysia. As the fruit are very sour, they are not eaten on their own but are thinly sliced and dried for use in cooking. Dried *assam gelugor* slices can be used as a substitute for tamarind pulp.

BLACK BEANS These small oval shaped beans have black skins and light green-coloured flesh. They are dried and need to be soaked before use to reduce the cooking time. Before cooking, pick through the beans to remove any pebbles or withered beans.

BLACK GLUTINOUS RICE Also known as black sticky rice, sweet rice or *pulut hitam,* this natural rice is not really black in colour but rather purplish with uneven coloured grains. It has a distinct nutty flavour and is commonly used for making desserts. Soak for 1–2 hours before using.

CANDLENUTS Known as *buah keras* in Malay, these cream-coloured nuts are usually ground and used spice pastes and curries to bring out the pungency of the chillies and to thicken the gravy. Because of their high oil content, the nuts can go rancid rather quickly and it is best to store them in the refrigerator.

CARDAMOM Known in Malay as *buah pelaga,* these straw-coloured pods contain tiny black seeds which are highly fragrant and flavourful. The whole pods can be lightly bruised to release the seeds and heighten the flavour prior to use.

CINNAMON Known *kayu manis* in Malay, cinnamon comes from the inner bark of the cinnamon tree, which is native to Sri Lanka. It has a sweet, penetrating aroma and is available in the form of sticks or powder. A versatile spice, cinnamon can be used in both sweet and savoury preparations.

CLOVES Known as *bunga chengkih* in Malay, cloves are used in many cuisines around the world. They can be used either whole or in ground form, but should be used sparingly because they have an extremely strong flavour.

CORIANDER LEAVES (CILANTRO)
Also known as Chinese parsley and *ketumbar* in Malay, coriander has a strong distinctive aroma. All parts of the plant are edible, including the root, but the fresh leaves and the dried seeds are most commonly used. Coriander leaves can be cooked or used raw as a garnish.

DILL Known also as dill weed, this herb has light wiry leaves that grow in clusters. Dill has a distinctive fennel and aniseed flavour and goes well as a garnish for seafood dishes. Local dill (top) has a milder flavour compared to western dill (below).

GALANGAL Also known as blue ginger, wild ginger, *lengkuas*, *kha* and *laos*, galangal is a rhizome of the ginger family. It is recognisable by its faintly pink-coloured skin and cream-coloured flesh. Galangal has a distinct, warm aroma and a sharp taste. Peel the thin skin, then slice before grinding or pounding with other spices.

KAFFIR LIME LEAVES Also known as *daun limau purut* or *makroot* leaf, these stiff, dark green and glossy leaves can be easily identified as they look like two leaves joined end to end. They are highly fragrant, but when using whole, crushing or tearing them will yield more flavour. The fresh leaves store well in the freezer.

LEMON GRASS Known locally by its Malay name, *serai*, this fragrant, lemon-scented stem grows in clumps with long, thin green leaves. These leaves are usually discarded, leaving the bulbous stem, which can be pounded, ground, smashed or sliced to release its flavour before cooking.

LOCAL CELERY Known as *daun soup* in Malay, this herb is sometimes confused with coriander leaves (cilantro), but it can be distinguished by its thicker stems and larger, flatter leaves. It is not as fragrant as coriander and is typically used as a garnish. It is a fraction the size of western celery.

MUSTARD SEEDS Known as *biji sawi* in Malay, it is the black and brown variety of mustard seed that is most commonly used in Asian cooking. These small round seeds have a sharp, fiery flavour. They can be used whole or pounded with other spices to make curry powders or pastes.

PALM SUGAR Known locally as *gula melaka,* this variety of palm sugar is made from the sap of the coconut tree. The sap is tapped from the tree, then boiled to thicken and placed into bamboo tubes to solidify. In Eurasian cooking, it is typically made into syrup to flavour desserts. Strain the syrup to remove any impurities before using.

PANDAN LEAF Also known as screwpine leaves or *daun pandan,* these leaves add a floral aroma to sweet and savoury dishes. When adding whole to dishes, wipe clean, then tie into a knot to keep the leaves together while bruising them to release their flavours.

PRAWN (SHRIMP) PASTE, DRIED (BELACAN) Also known as *terasi* or *kapi*, dried prawn paste is a common ingredient used in many South East Asian cuisines. Sold as blocks or discs, this pungent paste is made by fermenting tiny prawns or *gerago*. It can be pink or dark brown in colour. Before using, roast by dry-frying in a wok.

PRESERVED SOY BEAN PASTE Known locally as *taucheo*, this flavourful paste is made by fermenting soy beans with salt. Although referred to as a paste, it is available with the beans whole, lightly mashed or made into a paste. In Eurasian cooking, it is usually mashed with other ingredients into a paste and stir-fried until fragrant.

SAGO Traditionally made from the starch extracted from the sago palm, sago comes in the form of white beads that may vary in size. In Eurasian desserts, small sago pearls are used. The pearls are opaque white before cooking but turn translucent once cooked. Cooked sago is slightly chewy but otherwise tasteless, hence syrup is added for flavour.

SALTED VEGETABLE (KIAM CHYE) This is the salted and pickled inner stem of the mustard green. It has a lovely crunchy texture which is largely maintained even after cooking. Salted vegetable is used to flavour stir-fries, soups and stews and can also be thinly sliced and served as an appetiser. Rinse and soak in water for at least 30 minutes to remove excess salt before use.

SEMOLINA Semolina is a pale yellow-coloured flour, ground from high-protein durum wheat. It is most commonly recognised as an ingredient used in making pasta, but can also be used to make other doughs as well as cakes. In Eurasian cooking, semolina is synonymous with making sugee cake.

SPRING ONION (SCALLION) Known locally as *daun bawang,* this is the young onion plant, harvested before the bulb swells to become an onion. It has a light, sweet flavour and both the shoots and leaves are used. Spring onion makes an excellent garnish for soups, fried dishes and roasts.

STAR ANISE Easily recognisable by its shape resembling a star, this spice has a strong aniseed flavour and is typically used whole in stews and curries. Use sparingly, as indicated in the recipe, to avoid altering the taste of the dish.

SWEET POTATOES Known also by its Malay name, *keledek,* this large, starchy tuberous root is a favourite ingredient in many South East Asian sweets and desserts. Orange flesh sweet potatoes are the most common variety, but purple flesh sweet potatoes are sometimes available. They can be used interchangeably.

TAMARIND PULP Extracted from the pods of the tamarind tree, this pulp is popularly used as a souring agent in cooking. It is sold still in their pods or packed into blocks. To use, the pulp must first be mixed with water. To do this, place both pulp and water in a bowl and use your fingers to knead the pulp until it dissolves. Strain the liquid to remove any seeds or fibre.

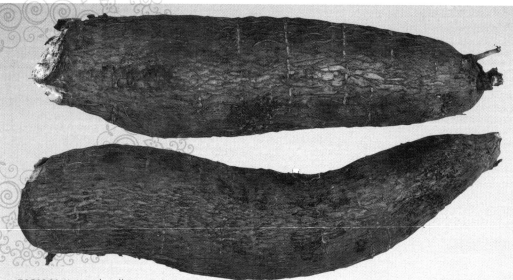

TAPIOCA Known locally as tapioca or *ubi kayu*, this is actually the root of the cassava plant. It is sometimes confused with the sweet potato but can be distinguished from the latter by its rough woody skin. Tapioca has a delicate flavour and can be used in both sweet and savoury preparations. In South East Asian cooking, it is popularly used in desserts.

TURMERIC Known locally as *kunyit*, this member of the ginger family is easily identified by its bright yellow-orange flesh. It can be used fresh and in powder form. To use fresh, scrape off the thin skin and slice thinly or as required in the recipe. Ground turmeric is a common ingredient in many spice mixtures.

YAM BEAN Known locally as *bangkwang*, this tuber has a thin light brown skin that can be easily peeled off to reveal its creamy white and crunchy flesh. Yam bean can be eaten raw or cooked, and it retains its sweetness and crunchy texture even after cooking.

WHITE WHEAT (TERIGU) The bran of white wheat is lighter in colour than traditional red wheat, hence its name. In South East Asia, white wheat, or *terigu* as it is most commonly known, is almost synonymous with the dessert *bubur terigu*, in which it is the main ingredient.

MENU SUGGESTIONS

Christmas Celebration
Cucumber Salad (page 40)
Calamari Fritters (page 46)
Mulligatawny (page 60)
Curry Debal (page 154)
Pot Roast Beef (page 158)
Kristang Stew (page 82)
Feng Curry (page 100)
Curry Moolie (page 120)
Prawn Chilli Garam (page 110)
Pineapple Tarts (page 142)
Sugee Cake (page 166)

New Year Celebration
Sambal Acar Nanas (page 36)
Fried Aubergines (page 72)
Tim Soup (page 56)
Meaty Cutlets (page 42)
Curry Debal (page 154)
Chap Chye (page 68)
Pineapple Prawn Curry (page 112)
Prawn Bostador (page 160)
Bubor Terigu (page 132)
Sago Gula Melaka (page 126)

Birthday Celebration
Chap Chye (page 68)
Sambal Acar Nenas (page 36)
Birthday Mee (page 152)
Curry Debal (page 154)
Baked Broccoli and Cauliflower (page 156)
Permenta Fried Prawns (page 114)
Babi Assam (page 96)
Beef Steak (page 104)
Watermelon, Honeydew and Sago
   in Coconut Milk (page 128)
Sugee Cake (page 166)

Home Party
Acar Timun Serani (page 34)
Seybak (page 50)
Prawn Ball Soup (page 58)
Aubergine Patchri (page 70)
Dhall Kristang (page 80)
Porku Tambreyno (page 94)
Ikan Chuan Chuan (page 122)
Sotong Black (page 116)
Pulut Hitam (page 130)

Tea Party
Calamari Fritters (page 46)
Devil Wings (page 48)
Pang Susie (page 162)
Kueh Ko Chee (page 146)
Kueh Bingka (page 138)
Bread Pudding (page 144)
Pulut Hitam (page 130)

WEIGHTS & MEASURES

Quantities for this book are given in Metric, Imperial and American (spoon) measures.
Standard spoon and cup measurements used are: 1 tsp = 5 ml, 1 Tbsp = 15 ml, 1 cup = 250 ml.
All measures are level unless otherwise stated.

Liquid and Volume Measures

Metric	Imperial	American
5 ml	1/6 fl oz	1 teaspoon
10 ml	1/3 fl oz	1 dessertspoon
15 ml	1/2 fl oz	1 tablespoon
60 ml	2 fl oz	1/4 cup (4 tablespoons)
85 ml	2 1/2 fl oz	1/3 cup
90 ml	3 fl oz	3/8 cup (6 tablespoons)
125 ml	4 fl oz	1/2 cup
180 ml	6 fl oz	3/4 cup
250 ml	8 fl oz	1 cup
300 ml	10 fl oz (1/2 pint)	1 1/4 cups
375 ml	12 fl oz	1 1/2 cups
435 ml	14 fl oz	1 3/4 cups
500 ml	16 fl oz	2 cups
625 ml	20 fl oz (1 pint)	2 1/2 cups
750 ml	24 fl oz (1 1/5 pints)	3 cups
1 litre	32 fl oz (1 3/5 pints)	4 cups
1.25 litres	40 fl oz (2 pints)	5 cups
1.5 litres	48 fl oz (2 2/5 pints)	6 cups
2.5 litres	80 fl oz (4 pints)	10 cups

Dry Measures

Metric	Imperial
30 grams	1 ounce
45 grams	1 1/2 ounces
55 grams	2 ounces
70 grams	2 1/2 ounces
85 grams	3 ounces
100 grams	3 1/2 ounces
110 grams	4 ounces
125 grams	4 1/2 ounces
140 grams	5 ounces
280 grams	10 ounces
450 grams	16 ounces (1 pound)
500 grams	1 pound, 1 1/2 ounces
700 grams	1 1/2 pounds
800 grams	1 3/4 pounds
1 kilogram	2 pounds, 3 ounces
1.5 kilograms	3 pounds, 4 1/2 ounces
2 kilograms	4 pounds, 6 ounces

Oven Temperature

	°C	°F	Gas Regulo
Very slow	120	250	1
Slow	150	300	2
Moderately slow	160	325	3
Moderate	180	350	4
Moderately hot	190/200	370/400	5/6
Hot	210/220	410/440	6/7
Very hot	230	450	8
Super hot	250/290	475/550	9/10

Length

Metric	Imperial
0.5 cm	1/4 inch
1 cm	1/2 inch
1.5 cm	3/4 inch
2.5 cm	1 inch

RESOURCES

Books

Braga-Blake, Myrna. *Singapore Eurasians: Memories and Hopes.* Singapore: Times Editions, 1992.

Hutton, Wendy. *The Food Of Love: Four Centuries of East-West Cuisine.* Singapore: Marshall Cavendish Cuisine, 2008

Jarnagin, Laura. ed. "The Making of the Luso-Asian World: Intricacies of Engagement", Portuguese and Luso-Asian Legacies in Southeast Asia, 1511–2011. Volume 1. Singapore: Institute of Southeast Asian Studies, 2011.

O'donovan, Patricius. *Jungles Are Never Neutral: War-Time in Bahau: An Extraordinary Story of Exile and Survival: The Diaries of Brother O'Donovan FSC.* Ipoh, Malaysia: Media Masters Publishing, 2008.

Scully, Valerie and Zuzarte, Catherine. *The Most Comprehensive Eurasian Heritage Dictionary: Kristang-English, English-Kristang.* Singapore: SNP Reference, c2004.

Museums

Asian Civilisations Museum
1 Empress Place
Singapore 179555
www.acm.org.sg

Eurasian Heritage Centre
Eurasian Community House
139 Ceylon Road
Singapore 429744
www.eurasians.org.sg

National Museum of Singapore
93 Stamford Road
Singapore 178897
www.nationalmuseum.sg

INDEX

PHOTO CREDITS

All photographs by Hongde Photography except as indicated below:

Bernard Go: pages 6 (bottom left: stack of plates), 10 (right: staircase at the Eurasian Association building), 79 (left: Eurasian dishes), 107 (right: a Eurasian feast) and 125 (left: *pang susie* buns waiting to be put into the oven)

John Randall Collection/National Archives of Singapore: page 18

Reproduced with permission from Mary Klass/National Archives of Singapore: page 21

Ministry of Information, Communications and the Arts/National Archives of Singapore: Back cover (a cooking competition, 1974)

National Archives of Singapore: pages 13–17

National Museum of Singapore Collection/National Archives of Singapore: Second inset image on the front cover (portrait of a Eurasian family, circa 1900)

The Pereira family: Third inset image (cooking in Kampong Serani, circa 1950) and fourth inset image (a family gathering, circa 1980s) on the front cover, pages 19, 22–23, 25–26

Singapore Recreation Club/National Archives of Singapore: First inset image on the front cover (club members at a Singapore Girls' Sports Club party, circa 1950.), pages 20 and 27

ABOUT THE AUTHOR

Quentin Pereira

Quentin Pereira, best known as the Skinny Chef, is a leading name when it comes to Eurasian cuisine. He set up Quentin's The Eurasian Restaurant giving Eurasian fare representation in Singapore's food-scape. He learned the art of cooking from his parents and grandparents and now shares well-kept family recipe secrets at his restaurant to impart his knowledge of Eurasian dishes to others. As a leading name in Eurasian cuisine, he has in numerous instances represented the Eurasian community with his cooking at such events as the People Association's Chingay celebrations, National Heritage Board's Heritage Fest and Overseas Singapore Unit's Singapore Day in Shanghai, China, organised by the Prime Minister's Office.